Effective Prayers for Body, Soul and Spirit

HEALING THE WHOLE MAN HANDBOOK

JOAN HUNTER

WHITAKER
HOUSE

Medical references and information came from many different sources. More detailed descriptions of disease processes may be found by accessing sites such as: National Institute of Health/US Department of Health and Human Services: www.nih.gov; US National Library of Medicine: www.medlineplus.gov, which offers easy-to-read health information in plain language to low-vision viewers; Mayo Clinic: www.mayoclinic.com; A.D.A.M.'s Health Illustrated Medical Encyclopedia at: http://www.nlm.nih.gov/medlineplus/encyclopedia.html; www.healthline.com; www.health.msn.com

HEALING THE WHOLE MAN HANDBOOK:
Effective Prayers for Body, Soul, and Spirit
Revised Edition

Joan Hunter Ministries
P.O. Box 1072
Pinehurst, TX 77362
www.joanhunter.org

ISBN-13: 978-0-88368-815-1
ISBN-10: 0-88368-815-8
Printed in the United States of America
© 2005, 2006 by Joan Hunter

Whitaker House
1030 Hunt Valley Circle
New Kensington, PA 15068
www.whitakerhouse.com

Library of Congress Cataloging-in-Publication Data

Hunter, Joan, 1953–
   Healing the whole man handbook : effective prayers for the body, soul, and spirit / Joan Hunter. — Rev. ed.
      p. cm.
   Summary: "Lists a variety of diseases and medical conditions with instructions on how to pray specifically for each one and also gives general tips for healing ministry"—Provided by publisher.
   Includes index.
   ISBN-13: 978-0-88368-815-1 (trade pbk. : alk. paper)
   ISBN-10: 0-88368-815-8 (trade pbk. : alk. paper)   1. Spiritual healing. I. Title.
   BT732.5.H796 2006
   234'.13—dc22   2006016873

5 6 7 8 9 10 11 12 **UJ** 15 14 13 12 11 10

This Book is dedicated to all the believers who have been faithfully doing the works of Jesus throughout the years. It is also dedicated to the believers who will catch the vision contained in this book and run with it.

ACKNOWLEDGEMENTS:

Naida Johnson, RN, CWS, FCCWS, for her devotion
to this book and the many hours she has spent
in the editing of this book.

A special thank you to

Spice Lussier, NMD, for her help and advice in *Healing the Whole Man Handbook.*

I would also like to thank those who contributed to this book in so many other ways, the hundreds of believers who have learned and applied the principles of the teachings, as well as those who have contributed information from their experiences in the area of healing.

I would like to make it understood that I am in no way associated with the medical or physiological profession. I do not claim to treat or diagnose any disease or illness. I do not offer the information included in this book as a substitute for medical advice or treatment. It is for your general knowledge only. I also do not take responsibility for any individual's disease or illness nor am I responsible for their healing. I offer no guarantee that anyone will be healed or that any disease or illness will be prevented.

I do, however, believe that we are spirit beings who have a soul and live in a body according to 1 Thessalonians 5:23. I also believe that most problems that manifest in the soul and body have a spiritual root and that Jesus paid the price for our healing (Isaiah 53:5, 1 Peter 2:24).

I do believe God heals today because He is the same yesterday, today, and tomorrow.

Contents

Introduction

*E*phesians 1:17–19 NKJV states,

> *That the God of our Lord Jesus Christ, the Father of glory, may give to you the spirit of wisdom and revelation in the knowledge of Him, the eyes of your understanding being enlightened; that you may know what is the hope of His calling, what are the riches of the glory of His inheritance in the saints, and what is the exceeding greatness of His power toward us who believe, according to the working of His mighty power.*

It is God's plan that our eyes be opened to everything that He has for us in ministry as well as every other area of life. It is His plan that the eyes of our understanding be enlightened to those we should be ministering to as well. It is essential we understand what God has called us to say and do each and every day.

The book of Mark does not say that those who believe will lay hands on the sick and "upon occasion" they may recover. No, it states, *"They **will** lay hands on the sick, and they **will** recover"* (Mark 16:18 NKJV, emphasis added).

9

Most Christians believe that God can heal, no matter what denomination they belong to or what church they attend. So why aren't people being healed within the church around the world? Why aren't Christians laying hands on the sick and seeing them recover?

The Scripture says, *"These signs will follow those who believe"* (Mark 16:17 NKJV). It could be interpreted as those who believe that God will actually use them, those who believe God's Word is for them personally, and those who believe that God will move through them as they obey His Word. Those who believe the Word understand the hope of the calling on their lives and know that God will move through them to accomplish the miraculous.

I remember the day I realized God could use me, not because I was Charles and Frances Hunter's daughter, not because I went to ORU (Oral Roberts University), or because of any ability of my own. I knew He could use me because I believed His Word was true and at that point the possibilities for my life became limitless through faith in God.

If God can use me, He can use you, too. If God can heal me from the top of my head to the soles of my feet, He can heal you. If He can restore my broken heart and wounded spirit, He can heal yours as well. God can do through you what He has done through me and even more. Don't put limits on what God can do for you or through you because of your particular circumstances. Instead, believe that you have a limitless God, that His Word is true, and that it is His plan to use you to change lives.

CHAPTER 1

Why Am I Sick?

hy am I sick? This question is asked by everyone including professionals, housewives, and even pastors. There is only one answer: sin! Think about it. Was there sickness in the garden of Eden? Sin causes sickness. However, it does not have to be your personal sin. Hebrews 11:4 tells us that Abel was a righteous man, but we know he died because of his brother's sin. According to the Word of God, the sins of the fathers are passed down to the third and fourth generations (Exodus 34:7).

When Jesus spoke to the crippled man who was healed, He confirmed that sin causes sickness. Afterward Jesus found him in the temple, and said to him, *"See, you are well again. Stop sinning or something worse may happen to you"* (John 5:14). Paul confirmed this also when he was talking to Christians about the way they took communion: *"That is why many among you are weak and sick, and a number of you have fallen asleep"* (1 Corinthians 11:30).

There are some who believe that sin is not the culprit and quote John: *"As he went along, he saw a man blind from birth. His disciples asked him, 'Rabbi, who sinned, this man or his parents, that he was born blind?' 'Neither this man nor his parents sinned,' said Jesus, 'but this happened so that the work of God might be displayed in his life'"* (John 9:1–3).

The disciples had been taught that sin caused sickness and that is why they asked the question. Jesus never denied that sin causes sickness. He just stated that in this particular case neither the afflicted man nor his parents sinned, but this blindness existed so the work of God might be displayed.

Some people have been taught that their sickness is from God and it somehow brings glory to God. If you hold on to this distorted thinking, then would it not bring Him more glory if you were even sicker? This way of thinking is contrary to Jesus' teaching and would contradict Jesus' commissioning of His disciples. *"He called his twelve disciples to him and gave them authority to drive out evil spirits and to heal every disease and sickness"* (Matthew 10:1). The word *"every"* means all diseases and sicknesses, excluding none.

> *Jesus gave His disciples authority to heal every disease.*

Some Christians have been taught that the healing ministry of the church ceased when the last of the original twelve disciples died. I count myself among His disciples and I agree with the early church. I believe Jesus still heals today. I have seen countless types of disease and illness healed in the name of Jesus and I know that the healing power of God is as real an experience today as during the lives of the apostles. I believe the acts of the Holy Spirit still occur today wherever the kingdom of God is being preached and the people believe. *"When Jesus had called the Twelve together, he gave them power and authority to drive out all demons and to cure diseases, and he sent them out to preach the king-dom of God and to heal the sick"* (Luke 9:1–2).

Finally, there is a group of people who believe that God still heals today, but they do not believe that God wants to heal them or use them to minister healing to others. They believe this for any number of reasons, none of which are true. The truth is, God is willing to heal anyone who believes, as Jesus showed in Matthew: *"Jesus reached out his hand and touched the man. 'I am willing,' he said. 'Be clean!' Immediately he was cured of his leprosy"* (Matthew 8:3).

Sin causes sickness but Jesus came to heal, and He still heals today. Jesus will not only heal you, He will also use you to minister healing to others by faith.

CHAPTER 2

The Call on Your Life

*I*n the next few chapters of this book, you will see terms like *call, calling, vision,* or *gifting.* The *call* or *calling* on your life refers to the purposes and destiny that God placed within you when you were born. Your *calling* exists in both the past and present tenses and will be referred to in that manner. Your call is alive and makes up part of your identity whether you are currently fulfilling it or whether it is still hidden within your heart.

Your *vision,* as referred to in this book, is the present and future tense fulfillment of the call on your life. It is the potential that will happen when your calling becomes reality. It is also God-given and thus carries His life in it.

And finally your *giftings* are your God-given abilities, both natural and supernatural through Jesus to fulfill the vision He has given you. These gifts exist in the past, present, and future tense and will grow in both strength and number to ensure the fulfillment of your vision.

Before you begin to minister healing to others through the prayers in this book, it is important to remember that God wants us to know the hope of His calling (Ephesians 1:18). God has a purpose for each believer's life. The passion you feel for ministry was put within you by God. I believe that you are reading this book now to help fulfill God's call on your life. You may not answer God's call through full-time ministry in a Christian organization, but God has given you a ministry (2 Corinthians 5:18).

So my question to you is, "Do you know the call that God has given you?" You should be able to answer the question, "What is God's purpose for your life?" without doubt or hesitation. Think about your purpose, about what God has called you to accomplish, and about His plan for your life. Unless that purpose is alive in your heart and becomes the central motivation of your daily walk, how can you be sure you are accomplishing God's will?

> *The passion you feel for ministry was put within you by God.*

If you are unaware of your calling and purpose, you may be in danger of picking up the calling of someone else. Consider these questions: Have you ever envied someone else's calling? Do you want what someone else has?

I meet people everywhere who are seeking the calling of others and have missed their own. I have actually met people who want to be a Frances Hunter. They try to do everything just like she did because they want to have her calling.

I have friends who have attempted to mimic the mannerisms of Christian leaders right down to their hand motions. Some have gone so far as to copy Billy Graham's North Carolina accent, the way he holds his Bible, and many of his phrases. God's plan, however, was to make each of us unique members of the same body of Christ (1 Corinthians 12:12–14; Ephesians 4:16). He does not tell us to conform to each other, but rather to be conformed to the image of His Son (Romans 8:29). We are not to have the mind of Frances Hunter or Billy Graham. We are to have the mind of Jesus Christ (1 Corinthians 2:16).

Be who God intended you to be and do what God made you to do (1 Corinthians 12:4–12; Romans 12:3–8). Don't become a living Xeroxed copy of someone else's calling. Wouldn't it be sad to get to heaven and discover you spent your life doing something other than what God had called you to do? It is possible.

There is a man who had such an experience and his story is life-changing. While this man was in law school, the Lord called him and his new bride to be missionaries in Africa. They said, "Yes, Lord, we'll go!" and began raising the necessary funds. Just as they were ready to leave for the mission field, they discovered she was pregnant. Knowing that the area to which they were called was a remote jungle, friends and family advised them to have the baby in the United States before moving to Africa.

They delayed their departure. Their blessing from God, a son, needed six months of medical care after his birth. Since the medical expenses used up their savings, the man accepted a job in a law firm in order to pay the bills. During his career as a very successful Christian businessman, he led many people to a relationship with the Lord wherever he went. When he received the baptism of the Holy Spirit, he became on fire for God! As one of the leaders in Florida's Full Gospel Businessmen, he led thousands of people to the Lord, went on many missions trips, funded and planted many churches, and raised all of his sons into ministry. In addition to all of that, each year he sent tens of thousands of dollars to missionaries in Africa, because that area was always on his heart.

After he retired, he was rocking on the porch of his large home overlooking the river, thanking the Lord for His blessings and for the great things God had done through him. Suddenly, God interrupted his train of thought. Clearly the voice of the Lord said, "I never called you to do any of this. I called you to be a missionary in Africa. No one would have known you, but you would have done what I called you to do. If you had obeyed me, it would not have been the same. Your son would not have become ill and you would not have gone through these trials. I called you to be a missionary in Africa."

Answer the call that God places on your life.

This man had always known that something was missing in his life and at that moment, he realized exactly what it was. It so profoundly touched him that wherever he goes, he tells everyone who will listen: "Answer the call that God places on your life."

Yes, God does have a specific purpose and plan for your life. He wants you to fulfill what He called you to do. When you hear, *"Well done, good and faithful servant"* (Matthew 25:21), it will be because you accomplished what God wanted you to, not because you did what you thought or hoped He wanted you to do.

God's purpose for your life is for you alone and nobody else on earth can accomplish it in the way that you can. God made each of us for a specific purpose. *"For we are God's workmanship, created in Christ Jesus to do good works, which God prepared in advance for us to do"* (Ephesians 2:10).

If God calls you to something that you don't feel you have the ability to accomplish, don't let that keep you from answering

17

His call. For example, if you had to choose between Peter and Paul as the apostle to the Jews and the Gentiles, which would you pick? Wouldn't it have made more sense to send Paul to the Jews? He was a Hebrew of Hebrews and an educated Pharisee who could talk with them intelligently. In the same respect, wouldn't it make more sense to send Peter, the uneducated fisherman, to the Gentiles?

But God is not limited to man's wisdom (James 3:14–18; 1 Corinthians 2:4). God sent Paul to the Gentiles and Peter to the Jews. God called Peter and Paul according to His purpose and His plan, so that they would accomplish the tasks set before them by His power and by His grace alone.

You can help identify the true call on your life by looking at the goals you have set in your heart. If your goals are to promote yourself, make money, have a place of leadership, arrive at a level of notoriety, or gain importance and prestige before men, then those goals are not from God (Acts 8:9–24). Goals that flow out of a selfish, self-centered mind-set can't be aligned with the eternal purposes of God. Your goals should be designed for the benefit of others. God-given goals will focus on the eternal destiny of souls and the complete fulfillment of God's purposes in the lives of others.

Ministry goals will not be about you if they come from God. Jesus was offered the whole world and turned it down. He was offered a high position and refused it (Matthew 4:1–11). He came for people. He specifically came for those who were lost, hurting, and in need. Our Lord Jesus emptied Himself and took on the form of a bondservant (Philippians 2:7 NKJV).

If God put the desire in your heart to reach people and change lives, you will find yourself following Jesus' example of sacrificial service (John 13:14; Matthew 19:16–22). If your calling is truly humble in appearance and doesn't exalt you, it may very well be from God (Matthew 7:13–14).

I have had the privilege to sit across the table from many successful Christian leaders who have told me to consistently choose the road that is the most selfless. If you take the road that seems most likely to promote your own interests, you will find it leads to places other than where God intended you to go. You will be going around the mountain one more time to find God's will for your life. There is a way to avoid this trip. Die!

The price to be paid to avoid these mistakes in direction is the death of "self." To walk in the fullness of the anointing, which is the empowerment of your calling, your natural "fleshly" man must go to the cross and die. The resurrection power of God cannot continually flow through uncrucified flesh (Philippians 3:9–11).

I often meet people who are ready for every part of ministry except death to self. They believe they have already died. They do not fully understand what it means to live for God rather than for self (Galatians 2:19–20). Simply put, it means that your "self" does not live anymore. *"For where you have envy and selfish ambition, there you find disorder and every evil practice"* (James 3:16).

If you live each day by your own selfish will and natural desires, you will bring disorder and evil works with you wherever you go. You may say, "But I'm anointed, I'm powerful. I lay hands on the sick and they recover. I prophesy. I cast out demons." *"Many will say to me on that day, 'Lord, Lord, did we not prophesy in your name, and in your name drive out demons and perform many miracles? Then I will tell them plainly, 'I never knew you. Away from me, you evildoers!'"* (Mathew 7:22–23).

Are your motives for yourself or for His sheep? When Jesus appeared to Peter after His resurrection, He told Peter to feed and take care of His sheep (John 21:15-17). He wanted him to understand that whatever he did for His sheep, it was as if he did it for Him. It is true for us also. When we minister to His sheep, we are ministering to Him (Matthew 25:40).

If you are unsure of the call on your life, seek God for it. God did not make you and then leave you without direction and purpose. He has placed your calling within your heart when He formed you and placed you in your mother's womb (Psalms 139:13–16). He had a purpose for your life from the beginning. Even the hairs on your head are numbered, and God has a wonderful plan for your future (Luke 12:7; Jeremiah 29:11). All you have to do is ask God to reveal to you what He has already placed in your heart. If you are unsure, ask Him now!

> *God had a purpose for your life from the beginning.*

Our own desires and plans, which tend to capture our attention and affection, often compete with His plan and purpose for our lives. Your heart may need to be circumcised from fleshly plans before you can truly see God's plan for your life. The only thing keeping you from doing what He called you to do is your "self." As you die to yourself and live for others, His plan for you will unfold rapidly. You will know in your spirit that you are on the right course and your life will take on a different motivation and value. Many of the desires in your heart for service to others will line up with God's purposes; and contentment will begin to fill your soul.

A Christian attorney in South Carolina was elected to the state House of Representatives. She was a conservative female candidate in a region where no conservative or woman had ever been elected in the history of the district. Her desire was to become a state judge. After a fair amount of politicking in the state's political circles, she became a judge. She won her race.

Because of her conservative views, she was given many high profile cases. She had to judge criminal cases where the death penalty was sometimes involved. She suddenly found that she had to make life and death rulings.

Unaware she was wrestling with the burdens of her position, her brother awoke in the middle of the night with an urgency to call her. He told her that the Lord had put something on his heart that he needed to share with her. He said, "It was the Lord's plan for you to be a judge. He is the one who opened the doors for you to have that position. He is the one who put the desire in your heart to be a judge, because He wanted a righteous judge that would ask Him what to do before dropping the gavel."

She started to cry as she said, "That's what I do. I was worried that it may have been out of my own desires that I became a judge and now people's lives are in my hands." This message was a confirmation that God had indeed called her to be a judge.

God gives you the desires of your heart because it is He who places those desires in your heart to start with.

CHAPTER 3

Your Gifts and His Supply

*M*ost believers are familiar with the Scripture that says, *"For God's gifts and his call are irrevocable"* (Romans 11:29). Do you know what that means? If you believe it has to do with your spiritual gifts and God's call on your life, you have been taught improperly by people who have taken this Scripture out of context. This Scripture has nothing to do with the spiritual gifts or the call of God on your life. One of the most dangerous things that you can do with Scripture is to separate the writings of Paul from the teachings of Jesus. This separation can tear the Word of God apart. The belief that this passage is about your gifts and calling is contrary to Jesus' parable of the talents.

This is the story of the Master who gave talents to his workers. Two of them took what was given to them and produced more, but one buried his talent and didn't do anything with it. In this parable the workers who produced more were given more, but the one who did nothing with his talent had it taken away from him (Matthew 25:14–30). This teaching of Jesus lines up with what I know about life.

I have seen through life experiences that people who have been given gifts and callings and don't use them, lose them. Take the time to read all of Romans 11 and you will see that this chapter is about salvation and the limited time that the Gentiles have for repentance. Romans 11:29 could read, "For God's gifts of salvation and His call for repentance to the Jews are irrevocable."

Do not deceive yourself by believing that you can choose to ignore God's call on your life and His spiritual gifts to you indefinitely before you act on them. The truth is, if you do not use them, you can lose them. *"From everyone who has been given much, much will be demanded; and from the one who has been entrusted with much, much more will be asked"* (Luke 12:48). If you have a call from God, don't wait to act on it unless He tells you to wait. You might be burying the talents God has given you to accomplish His plans.

With that understanding, consider what the Bible says, *"My God will meet all your needs according to his glorious riches in Christ Jesus"* (Philippians 4:19). If He is going to supply all your needs according to His riches in Christ Jesus, just what does that mean to you?

During the first Gulf War President Bush sent General Schwarzkopf overseas to free Kuwait from the invading Iraqis. President Bush told him, "Anything you need, just let me know."

Schwarzkopf could have called the President back and said, "You know, I would like a condo in Vail and I've always wanted to own a red Corvette. Two tickets to Disney World would also be nice so my family and I can spend some quality time together when this is all over."

President Bush would have responded, "What in the world are you talking about? Didn't you understand that I was referring to anything you needed to get the job done that I sent you to do?

All you have to do is just ask me, and I will make sure you have it."

You will not be able to get to heaven and say, "Oh God! If You had just given me $10,000,000, I would have been able to do so much more for You. Or, if You had just given me this or that, I would have accomplished so much more."

You already have what you need to accomplish the task He has called you to do, or He will supply it as you request it. If you don't have what you need to complete the task, then either you are not doing what God sent you to do, you have not asked Him for His help, or it is not His timing.

It is, however, not uncommon for a person to have to live outside their own abilities or comfort zone before His supply becomes a reality. No matter what your circumstances are like, do not limit God to your own abilities or by your own thinking. Ephesians 3:20 says, *"Now to him who is able to do immeasurably more than all we ask or imagine, according to his power that is at work within us."*

> *God has given you what you need to accomplish your task*

When God establishes a vision, His provision will always be there to accomplish what He has planned. He can and will supply all that you need to fulfill the call on your life.

CHAPTER 4

Vision and the Motivations of the Heart

hen a long distance runner runs a race, he knows his goal is to cross the finish line. He knows the finish line is there when he starts the race. He also knows it is there while he is running the race, but he can't see it because it is many miles away. The finish line is always in his sight even though it is not immediately visible.

This may best describe God's vision for your life. Your vision is the present and future tense fulfillment of God's call on your life. True visions are God-inspired and are full of His life. They come to pass through our spoken words and subsequent actions. These visions are essential to our very existence.

"Where there is no vision, the people perish" (Proverbs 29:18 KJV). Through life experiences, I have found sharing a God-given vision is an important way to ensure the calling is fulfilled. It is His purpose and plan for you to share your vision with others

(Habakkuk 2:2). If you are married, God will give you a vision that He wants you to share with your spouse.

There was a pastor in Africa who was called to be a missionary in the United States. He told his wife over and over that God had called him to be a missionary and establish a ministry in the USA. For months his wife repeatedly said, "No, no, no! I don't feel that we are called to go there." However, he kept sharing the vision with her until one day she said, "I know we are supposed to go to the U.S.!" She began to repeat the vision back to him because it was now alive in her heart also.

Share the vision that God has given you with others. If it is from God, it will stand. If it is not from God, it will not stand. But share your vision.

By now you should be aware of the call of God on your life or be seeking Him for the vision if you don't already have one. At this point, I must ask you to examine your heart and ask yourself these questions. What really drives you? What is in your heart of hearts? Do you understand the implications of this question? If God gave you a heart for souls and you are waiting to collect enough money to go overseas, but you don't have enough compassion to go across the street to minister to the lost, is your drive really for souls or is it for a mission overseas?

> *Share the vision that God has given you with others.*

Here is a different way of expressing the same concept. If you cannot go to your local grocery store and use the gift God has given you, what qualifies you to use it in the church? If it is not in your heart to touch people and see them healed in your local neighborhood, why should God open the door to greater opportunities?

Before you minister to others, it is essential that your heart's motivation be right before God. The Bible states in many places that when Jesus saw the crowds, He had compassion on them because they were like sheep without a shepherd (Matthew 9:36, 14:14, 20:34; Mark 1:41, Luke 7:13). Compassion is a driving force to ministry and is often misunderstood to be a soft mushy "sympathy" as described in Webster's Dictionary.

However, true compassion is an intense combination of both love and hate. Jesus had that kind of compassion. He loved the people with an uncompromised love and at the same time He hated the condition in which they were trapped. The word *compassion* in the Greek actually means to be stirred so strongly inside that your bowels are moved. The combination of great love and hatred creates an intense inner stirring. One empowers your spirit and the other motivates your soul into action.

It is important to understand the components of compassion and why we should be motivated in the same manner as our Lord. I don't feel that it is necessary to explain the nature of hate or what it feels like because everyone has experienced it. However, I have found that many have misunderstandings about the nature of love.

Some people have a misconception that the love that is in their heart is from themselves and that they have the ability to produce more. But this is not a reality. The truth is that the love we have did not come from us, it came from God. It was in the beginning, and it will be in the end. God is, so love is. *"God is love"* (1 John 4:16).

Paul's prayer to the Ephesians was: *"I pray that you, being rooted and established in love, may have power, together with all the saints, to grasp how wide and long and high and deep is the love of Christ, and to know this love* [by experience] *that surpasses knowledge—that*

27

you may be filled to the measure of all the fullness of God" (Ephesians 3:17–19).

I believe it will take an eternity for me to fully comprehend all that love encompasses. Each day of my life, I gain a greater understanding of who God is; and as I do, I will experience His love with more intensity and purity.

This passage of Scripture is all about love:

> *If I speak in the tongues of men and of angels, but have not love, I am only a resounding gong or a clanging cymbal. If I have the gift of prophecy and can fathom all mysteries and all knowledge, and if I have a faith that can move mountains, but have not love, I am nothing. If I give all I possess to the poor and surrender my body to the flames, but have not love, I gain nothing. Love is patient, love is kind. It does not envy, it does not boast, it is not proud. It is not rude, it is not self-seeking, it is not easily angered, it keeps no record of wrongs. Love does not delight in evil but rejoices with the truth. It always protects, always trusts, always hopes, always perseveres. Love never fails.* (1 Corinthians 13:1–8)

If you do not have this passage memorized, I suggest you do so now. Read it until you can quote it anywhere at anytime. You can read it and know all the words. However, when these words become a revelation within your heart, they will change your life.

Unfortunately, it is possible to do all the amazing things in 1 Corinthians 13:1–3 without a motivation of love. Apparently, this is what has happened to some members of the church. Some parts of the modern church have drifted away from the lifestyle of love as it was exhibited by the early church. The first act of the New Testament church was to sell all of their excess property and give the proceeds to the poor.

When hurricane Ivan came through Florida, it destroyed some churches and tore the roofs off many others west of Tallahassee. Several churches located east of Tallahassee gave their building funds to the congregations of the damaged churches when they heard the church insurance policies would not cover the cost of the repairs. These churches were not concerned about denominational lines or doctrinal differences. They wanted to reach out to mend hearts and aid churches that were in need. They gave up the building funds they had accumulated over several years so others could have a building in which to worship God.

The Bible says that the world would know that we are Christians because of our love (John 13:35). Most people in the United States know enough about God's Word to be saved. However, they also know some questionable Christians and do not want to be like them. There are many things I could say about

> *The world will know we are Christians by our love.*

this subject but if you get nothing else out of this chapter, please remember this: love never fails. Love never fails. *Love never fails* (1 Corinthians 13:8).

When you do minister to someone and you have done nothing but love them, then....Love never fails. You may pray for someone who is not instantly healed. Remember that love never fails. God's call on your life will always be driven by a spirit of compassion. Love them and believe that love never fails. God is love. God never fails. Love never fails.

"And now these three remain faith, hope and love. But the greatest of these is love" (1 Corinthians 13:13).

CHAPTER 5

It's All about Relationships

*J*esus came that we might have life and have it more abundantly (John 10:10 NKJV).

Life is not about places or things; it is about our relationship and service to God as well as our relationships and service to His people. To confirm this fact in your life, assume you knew you were going home to be with the Lord at midnight tonight. What would you do differently between now and then? More than likely, places and things would lose their value and you would spend your remaining time with those people who mean the most to you.

When we become alienated in our relationships, our lives reflect the strain and our hearts can harden. This alienation can infiltrate slowly, but surely, into every area of our lives including our family, friends, church, and work, as well as our relationship with God. It is quite obvious that the most important relationship we have is with our Father.

In my travels I am quite surprised to see so many believers who have lost their intimacy with God. I am equally surprised to see so many believers in the church who have never known this intimacy at all. It is defined by a *"love that surpasses knowledge"* (Ephesians 3:19).

Christians who don't have an understanding of intimacy with God are frequently reading Christian books and going to Christian conferences searching for what is missing in their lives. There is nothing wrong with Christian books or conferences; but if you feel like there is something missing in your walk with God, maybe what you need is an alignment to His heart and His unconditional love. Then the Christian books and conferences will add to your walk instead of trying to replace what you feel is missing.

There are many reasons why we separate ourselves from God. Sin, unbelief, and disobedience are the most common reasons, and they are easily rectified by repentance, so I will not go into detail about them at this time. There is another reason that is less talked about, but seems to be very common. It is a separation through time by slowly hardening your heart toward God because He did not perform as you would have if you were God. You have been hurt or even angry with God so you hold unwritten things against Him while waiting for Him to correct them.

This may be best explained using the marriage relationship. It is not uncommon to minister to men and women who do not have the love for their spouses they once had. Over time a spouse did things wrong or did not meet expectations. Small hurts slowly added up. Eventually, hearts hardened and they no longer feel the love that was once the cornerstone of their marriage. The intimacy is gone.

Our response to these people is always the same. What could your spouse do to win back your love? I get many responses from "I am not quite sure," to a list of things that would fill a ream of paper. To this my response is always the same. Release your spouse of their debt!

The spouse most likely does not deserve to be released and has not done enough to win you back, but simply release them from what you are holding against them. Lay down the conditions that you have set in your heart for your spouse to meet. Lay them on the altar of God and simply love your spouse. Then make the declaration to give 100 percent of your heart back to your spouse. You do it just like this:

Prayer to Release Spouse

"I willingly lay down all the conditions that I am expecting my spouse to meet on the altar of God. I (your full Christian name) choose to give 100 percent of my heart to (your spouse's full Christian name) from this day forth."

I have watched many people do this very thing and the love they once had for their mates filled their hearts again. It is so interesting to hear the testimonies of the amazing changes that took place in their relationships when they got home.

> *God has called you to unconditional love.*

Unconditional love is what God has called you to. If you have anything other than unconditional love, then you are in contradiction to who He is and who He made you to be.

Many Christians do the same thing to God that they did in their relationships even though they know in their heart they don't have the right to hold anything against God. Yet many times we still do. We prayed and He did not answer our prayers the way we wanted or someone we loved died and we didn't understand why.

There are many reasons why we separate ourselves from God. However He will never separate Himself from us. *"Never will I leave you; never will I forsake you"* (Hebrews 13:5). Jesus came that we might be reconciled *to* God. *"All this is from God, who reconciled us to himself through Christ and gave us the ministry of reconciliation: that God was reconciling the world to himself in Christ, not counting men's sins against them. And he has committed to us the message of reconciliation"* (2 Corinthians 5:18–19).

> *God will never separate Himself from us.*

When you are ministering to others, you may need to lead them in this simple prayer of restoration. You may also need to say this same prayer. I have seen countless numbers of people say this prayer and a love for God filled their hearts again.

Prayer for Restoration

"Father, I willingly lay down on Your Altar all the conditions that I was expecting You to meet. I (your full Christian name) choose to give 100 percent of my heart to You from this day forth. I will be Your servant and You will be my God, in Jesus' name."

The other factors of sin, disobedience, and unbelief are easily corrected. For you to be healed, sin must be confessed and not hidden in your heart. God set a pattern for how often He is willing to forgive us our sins. *"If we confess our sins, he is faithful and just and will forgive us our sins and purify us from all unrighteousness"* (1 John 1:9).

"Then Peter came to Him and said, 'Lord, how often shall my brother sin against me, and I forgive him? Up to seven times?' Jesus said to him, 'I do not say to you, up to seven times, but up to seventy times seven'" (Matthew 18:21–22 NKJV). In the Greek, this passage can be interpreted "not seven times but seventy-seven times for the same sin in the same day." It is God's nature to forgive us without measure.

However, there is a condition to forgiveness. God will only forgive us with the measure that we forgive others. *"For if you forgive men when they sin against you, your heavenly Father will also forgive you. But if you do not forgive men their sins, your Father will not forgive your sins"* (Matthew 6:14-15). If you hold any unforgiveness towards anyone, then you cannot be forgiven.

Jesus explained it like this:

Therefore, the kingdom of heaven is like a king who wanted to settle accounts with his servants. As he began the settlement, a man who owed him ten thousand talents was brought to him. Since he was not able to pay, the master ordered that he and his wife and his children and all that he had be sold to repay the debt. The servant fell on his knees before him. "Be patient with me," he begged, "and I will pay back everything." The servant's master took pity on him, canceled the debt and let him go. But when that servant went out, he found one of his fellow servants who owed him a hundred denarii. He grabbed him and began to choke him. "Pay back what you owe me!" he demanded. His fellow servant fell to his knees and begged him, "Be patient with me, and I will pay you back." But he refused. Instead, he went off and had the man thrown into prison until he could pay the debt. When the other servants saw what had happened, they were greatly distressed and went and told their master everything that had happened. Then the master called the servant in. "You wicked servant," he said, "I canceled all that debt of yours because you begged me to. Shouldn't you have had mercy on your fellow servant just as I had on you?" In anger his master turned him over to the jailers to be tortured, until he should pay back all he owed. This is how my heavenly Father will treat each of you unless you forgive your brother from your heart. (Matthew 18:23–35)

You have been forgiven everything, but if you can't forgive others who have sinned against you, then you are acting contrary to God's nature and will be separated from God. This is the prayer to confess sins:

Prayer to Confess Sin

"Father, I have sinned. I confess my sin(s) of (<u>insert the sin(s) you committed</u>). I repent and turn from this. Forgive me of this sin. I choose to forgive those who have sinned against me. Father, I choose to forgive (<u>name of person who sinned against you</u>). What they did was sin. Take this sin from them and place it on the cross of Jesus and on the day of judgment I will not hold this sin against them. Even now they are free. Father, bless them."

Unbelief is another form of sin that separates us from God. The opposite of unbelief is faith. Each man on earth has been given a measure of faith according to the Word of God (Romans 12:3). You already have faith and you use it every day. If you are sitting down while you are reading this, then you applied your faith. You had faith the chair would hold you when you sat down.

Faith pleases God. Faith is believing. The things of God are just that simple. *"And without faith it is impossible to please God,*

35

because anyone who comes to him must believe that he exists and that he rewards those who earnestly seek him" (Hebrews 11:6).

Prayer to Confess Unbelief.

"Father, I have not applied the faith You have given me. I have allowed doubt and unbelief to enter in. I confess this as sin and choose to turn back to You. Forgive me for this sin, in Jesus' name."

Disobedience is another form of sin that also separates us from God. When God was calling Moses to lead the children of Israel out of Egypt, He allowed Moses to express his doubts and inabilities and He answered them all. However, when Moses said, "Send someone else," *"the Lord's anger burned against Moses"* (Exodus 4:14).

> *Faith pleases God. The things of God are that simple.*

God put up with Moses' doubt and inabilities but He would not allow disobedience. He does not allow it today. He will correct you because He loves you. *"The Lord disciplines those he loves"* (Hebrews 12:6). Understand that if God has called you to accomplish something, you must do it. To run from it will separate you from God, and your life will reflect the emptiness that is found in the children of disobedience.

There was a man at a church in Indiana who was in constant pain from a back injury caused by an auto accident twelve years before. He had received prayer many times with only limited results. After a few questions, I determined he was running from the call of God on his life. In fact, he had had the accident right after he told the Lord, "No." After being led

36

in the prayer of repentance for disobedience, he was instantly healed.

Prayer for Disobedience:

"Father, I have disobeyed Your Word and Your plan for my life. I repent and turn back to serving You alone. Forgive me this sin and place it on the cross of Jesus Christ. I am Your servant from this day forth."

Most believers know of the first and greatest commandment, but do you know the second? *"Love the Lord your God with all your heart and with all your soul and with all your mind. This is the first and greatest commandment. And the second is like it: Love your neighbor as yourself"* (Matthew 22:37–39).

Jesus was not telling us that the second commandment was similar to the first, but was like it as seen from a different perspective. If you don't love your neighbor as yourself, you are deceived when you say you love God. When Peter asked Jesus, *"And who is my neighbor?"* (Luke 10:29), Jesus responded with the story of the Good Samaritan (verses 30–37).

John confirmed this when he said, *"For anyone who does not love his brother, whom he has seen, cannot love God, whom he has not seen. And he has given us this command: Whoever loves God must also love his brother"* (1 John 4:20-21).

We are called to love everyone unconditionally. Jesus said, *"If you love those who love you, what reward will you get? Are not even the tax collectors doing that?"* (Matthew 5:46).

The tax collectors would sit by the gates of the wall that surrounded Jerusalem. If taxes were not paid, the tax collectors would not allow the person to enter the city to worship God or make offerings at the temple.

We sometimes hold debts that others owe us and we will not let them past the walls of our heart unless that debt is paid. Jesus told people who did that, they were no different than the tax collectors.

> *If you love those who love you, what credit is that to you? Even "sinners" love those who love them. And if you do good to those who are good to you, what credit is that to you? Even "sinners" do that. And if you lend to those from whom you expect repayment, what credit is that to you? Even "sinners" lend to "sinners," expecting to be repaid in full. But love your enemies, do good to them, and lend to them without expecting to get anything back. Then your reward will be great, and you will be sons of the Most High, because he is kind to the ungrateful and wicked. Be merciful, just as your Father is merciful. Do not judge, and you will not be judged. Do not condemn, and you will not be condemned. Forgive, and you will be forgiven. Give, and it will be given to you. A good measure, pressed down, shaken together and running over, will be poured into your lap. For with the measure you use, it will be measured to you.*
>
> (Luke 6:32–38)

God frees us from judgment and condemnation and He forgives us with the same measure we use towards others. If there is anyone in your life that you have been holding anything against, release them and be free. This is also true when you are praying for others. Lead them in repentance so that they may be free as well.

Matthew 22:39 states, *"Love your neighbor as yourself."* I am surprised at the number of Christians who don't love themselves. Not only do some Christians not love themselves, but I have met people who actually hated themselves. This is definitely a contradiction to who you are and who you are called to be. Self-hatred will eventually affect all relationships, including the one with your heavenly Father. Whether it entered your life through sin, disobedience, or just believing lies about you, the fruit of hate is always the same. Devastation!

When you act contrary to who God made you to be, you will not like the fruit of your labor and will eventually not like yourself. If these ungodly actions continue over a period of time without repentance; you will not only hate your actions, you will hate yourself for continuing in them.

Your self-hatred may be brought on by your own sins. However, in some cases, it could be brought on by the sins of others. For example, if you grew up in an ungodly household where there was yelling, backbiting, condemnation, and constant criticism; as an adult you may exhibit many of these same characteristics. If you continue these same behaviors, you will have a difficult time loving yourself.

Some people were abused as children. They may be able to forgive their abuser, but they often take on the false belief that they were the cause of the abuse. They believe that there was something wrong or different about them that caused them to feel responsible for what happened. I have even ministered to people in their late seventies who did not like themselves because they believed they were somehow responsible for the abuse they received sixty-five years before. Believing such a lie is very common among victims of abuse and will keep people from loving themselves and will make it difficult for them to give their heart fully to others.

The answer to these problems is always the same. It is the cross of Jesus Christ. All healing takes place at the cross. Whether it is because of sin, disobedience, ungodly habits, or believing a lie, the answer is always the same. The way to change from hating yourself to loving yourself is simply repentance. *Repentance* means change, to turn the other way. It means you no longer act contrary to who you are in your heart; it means you take your previous actions to the cross.

Prayer of Repentance

"Father, I have not acted in accordance to Your nature and I am upset with myself for these actions. They are sin. I repent and I will no longer continue to act this way. Father, take this sin from me, place it on the cross of Jesus Christ, and separate it from me. Forgive me of this sin and forgive my fathers of this same sin as well, in Jesus' name."

Some teach that you need to forgive yourself. This teaching is not found anywhere in the Bible. It is an "I" centered thinking that is contrary to the cross. It turns you inward to forgive yourself instead of turning you to the cross where you accept God's forgiveness of your sins through Jesus Christ. Once you repent, you become free of these sins and don't need to forgive yourself, as if you really could.

> *The answer to problems is always the cross of Jesus Christ.*

The Bible says to cast your cares upon Jesus *"because He cares for you"* (1 Peter 5:7). It is not uncommon to find people who are carrying the cares of their life and their circumstances on their own shoulders. This is a simple but effective prayer to free you from the burden of these things:

Prayer to Cast Cares on the Altar

"Father, I am carrying the burdens of my relationships and circumstances. I choose to lay all my cares, all my worries, all my fears, all things I cannot change on Your altar. Father, I lay my spouse on Your altar. Father, I lay my children on Your altar. Father, I lay my job, my finances on Your altar. Father, I lay (<u>name the circumstances that you cannot change</u>) on Your altar. You are my supply and You alone can move in my circumstances. I give these to You and trust You with them, in Jesus' name."

I have countless testimonies of people whose heavy hearts became lighter or who felt the weight of the world leave their shoulders after repeating this prayer. I quite often use this prayer for people who have upper back or shoulder pain.

Finally, remember when you are ministering to people, you are called to a ministry of reconciliation, which is all about relationships.

CHAPTER 6

Steps in Ministering

When you minister to people, what should you do first? Follow Jesus' example.

Step One: Ask the person what they want. The Bible says to *"give to the one who asks you"* (Matthew 5:42). Don't start praying for the person before you talk with them. Ask them what they want. The question isn't, "What do you want me to do for you?" It is, "What do you need Jesus to do for you?" or "What are you expecting from God?"

Jesus had been ministering all day when a blind man called out to Him. What did Jesus say? *"What do you want me to do for you?"* (Mark 10:51). Why did Jesus ask him what he wanted? Wasn't it obvious that a blind man would want his sight restored?

A.B. was a man in Florida who had been in the healing ministry for exactly one day. He had been praying for people and seeing them healed when a man came rolling up in a wheelchair. His legs were atrophied. They were very thin and obviously very weak. It was obvious that he had not walked in a long time, if at all. A.B. was really taken back and did not know how to pray for the crippled man. A.B. was willing, but in the back of his mind he thought, "I'm going to pray for this guy, Lord, and if he does not get out of this wheelchair, one of us is going to be really embarrassed and I am quite sure that person will be me."

Before A.B. could do anything, the man in the wheelchair asked, "Can you lead me into the baptism of the Holy Spirit?"

A.B. said, "Yes, I can do that." If the man in the wheelchair hadn't spoken up, A.B. would not have known what he wanted. A.B. would have started praying for his crippled legs.

Step two: Ask the person how long they have had the problem. A woman who had a bad back for over four years came to me for ministry. She had received prayer from many other people without being healed. When I asked what happened four years before, she explained that her husband had left her for his secretary. She was still very hurt and bitter about it. She was led in a prayer of forgiveness; she put her hurt feelings on the cross and she was healed instantly. In the book of Mark, *"Jesus asked the boy's father, 'How long has he been like this?'"* (Mark 9:21).

Step three: Look. You asked them what they wanted, but now you need to look them in the eyes. It is really that simple. *"The eye is the lamp of the body. If your eyes are good, your whole body will be full of light. But if your eyes are bad, your whole body will be full of darkness"* (Matthew 6:22–23).

Always look the person in the eye and be sure they look back at you. Peter and John did this. *"Peter looked straight at him, as did John. Then Peter said, 'Look at us!' So the man gave them his attention, expecting to get something from them"* (Acts 3:4–5). If the person you are ministering to closes their eyes, tell them to open them. If they turn their head away from you or will not look you in the eye, they might be afraid.

If you see fear, step back until they relax. Some people become uncomfortable if you stand closer than an arm's length away, as if that space is a "trust zone" which you have trespassed or "trust-passed." Also, be sure you are not standing between the person and an aisle or a door, their way out. Whether you are ministering to a man or a woman, if you still see fear, try getting down on one or both knees to minister. In this position you should no longer be a threat.

If you do not detect fear, but the person still will not look you in the eye, it may be that they have unconfessed sin. They may be in a dispute with the Lord or with His representatives (pastors, lay ministers, etc.) and may be holding judgments in their heart against them. *"Therefore confess your sins to each other and pray for each other so that you may be healed. The prayer of a righteous man is powerful and effective"* (James 5:16).

If they do not repent of the sin or release the judgment against the other person, what will happen while you are ministering to them? Most likely nothing, unless they repent! Help bring them to repentance. Remember, never break trust with someone who confesses sin. If you do, you can cause them great pain and can bring judgment upon yourself.

Also look for outward signs of internal conditions. People communicate with body language as well as with their words. Are their arms crossed in front of them? Are they overly nervous or lethargic? Are there any other outward signs? Pray for whatever they request; but as a responsible representative of Jesus Christ, stay alert to other possible problems also (Matthew 24:42–43).

Step four: Listen. When you ask the person what they want, listen carefully to what they are saying. Many times, the first words that come out of a person's mouth will tell you the root problem. But also listen for complaints, gripes, or words that reveal negative attitudes against someone. For instance, listen for signs of unforgiveness, judgments, and bitterness (unfulfilled revenge).

"See to it that no one misses the grace of God and that no bitter root grows up to cause trouble and defile many" (Hebrew 12:15). However, do not let them go into detail about their situation. It can weigh you down and may take you off track or in a direction that will not lead to healing.

You may find that many of the problems, which they claim were caused by other people, are the very problems that now live within themselves. This is especially true when they are in judgment of others. The only way anyone can set themselves up as a judge of someone else is to be in authority over them. People tend to become angry and lose patience with others when a similar sin exists within themselves. Otherwise, they would have compassion on another and hurt for them instead of judging them. When the Jewish men were about to stone a woman caught in adultery, Jesus said, *"If any one of you is without sin, let him be the first to throw a stone at her"* (John 8:7).

This does not mean that judgment of another person was inaccurate; but if the conclusion caused any emotion other than compassion, there may be things that need to be crucified such as anger, bitterness, unforgiveness, selfishness, or other sins. These things need to be handled, often before ministering healing for a disease process.

Listen for what they are truly seeking. Is there something that they are not saying? Many men have no idea what they are feeling at the time, much less how to communicate it.

There was a man whose wife had committed adultery and he was looking for help. He truly did not know what he wanted. He was full of anger. He did not understand the hurt and mixture of emotions that he was experiencing. He just wanted to get rid of the pain. He had already seen an attorney and had filed for divorce. That was not what he wanted because he really loved the woman. He just wanted the hurt to go away. He wanted somebody to help him through the pain so he could get back to a place of peace.

Three hours after receiving ministry, he had his wife under his arm and said to her, "I love you, and we will get through this together. No one will dishonor you while I am your husband. We will get through this."

<u>Step five</u>: Relax. You and the person you are ministering to need to relax. Whether it is the first time you have prayed for someone or the thousandth time, you need to be relaxed. Take a deep breath. You cannot make it happen in your own power. If you aren't at peace, it will be hard to minister peace to someone else.

There are several things you can do to help people relax before they receive ministry. Tell them to: "Take a deep breath and relax" or "Relax like you are in your easy chair at home." If they tell you that they have a serious disease or illness like breast cancer, you should always say, "That is easy." You will be amazed at how often people relax after they hear those three simple words.

Some Christians will start speaking in tongues, raising their hands, singing or praising God while you try to minister to them. Stop them and instruct them to put their hands down at their sides. This is not the time for them to pray or thank God. They will thank Him later. Some people believe that by doing all of these things, they will somehow motivate God to act on their behalf while others have been taught that this is the "spiritual" thing to do.

I am not saying you should not raise your hands in church or praise and worship God. However, when someone is receiving prayer, I have found much better results when the person gets out of God's way and allows Him to work. After they have received ministry, encourage them to thank Jesus and to praise God for their healing. God wants to heal everyone. People need to relax and receive His touch.

Step six: Wait on the Lord. When you wait on the Holy Spirit, three minutes can seem like a long time and five minutes may feel like forever. This is when most Christians in the healing ministry miss God. They take it on themselves to do all they can think of to do rather than wait on the leading of the Holy Spirit.

There have been occasions when I have waited on the Holy Spirit for what seemed like a very long time. He may not always show up immediately, but He always shows up. Sometimes I don't know what I am waiting for Him to do, but I know that the Lord will accomplish His will when I wait on Him. If you are praying for people in a church service, you probably cannot wait fifteen to twenty minutes, but you can arrange to meet with them later when you have more time. You should take all the time they need. Don't try to rush God or the person receiving ministry.

I believe the person I am praying for is the most important person in my life during that time of ministry. If there is one person or a hundred more people waiting for prayer, I give the person in front of me my time and full attention as the Spirit directs.

Final Step: Don't quit. If you pray for people who don't get instantly healed, don't quit. Jesus prayed more than once for people. He prayed twice for a blind man before he was totally

47

healed (Mark 8:22–25). So don't quit. If someone does not get healed the first time you pray for them, pray again. Keep praying and asking God what to do next. And remember, God's timing is perfect.

You should be familiar with the story in Acts:

One day Peter and John were going up to the temple at the time of prayer—at three in the afternoon. Now a man crippled from birth was being carried to the temple gate called Beautiful, where he was put every day to beg from those going into the temple courts. When he saw Peter and John about to enter, he asked them for money. Peter looked straight at him, as did John. Then Peter said, "Look at us!" So the man gave them his attention, expecting to get something from them. Then Peter said, "Silver or gold I do not have, but what I have I give you. In the name of Jesus Christ of Nazareth, walk." Taking him by the right hand, he helped him up, and instantly the man's feet and ankles became strong. He jumped to his feet and began to walk. Then he went with them into the temple courts, walking and jumping, and praising God. When all the people saw him walking and praising God, they recognized him as the same man who used to sit begging at the temple gate called Beautiful, and they were filled with wonder and amazement at what had happened to him.

(Acts 3:1–10)

Peter and John met this man when they were going into the temple courts. Did Jesus ever go into the temple courts? The four Gospels record that He went quite often. Verse 2 says, *"Now a man crippled from birth was being carried to the gate Beautiful, where he was put every day."* If he sat begging at the temple gate every day, why didn't Jesus heal him? If Jesus walked by this man before, why didn't He heal him?

48

There is timing and purpose for everything in God. *"There is a time for everything, and a season for every activity under heaven"* (Ecclesiastes 3:1), including *"a time to heal"* (verse 3).

That particular day was God's chosen day for a miracle. Peter and John were there, and they followed God's plan. The crippled man was healed, and many came to the Lord because of his testimony. There is a perfect time for each healing and that timing will always bring glory to God.

This is all very simple. It is easy. These are basic steps that you need to practice when ministering healing to people. Don't be afraid to use the common sense and good judgment the Lord gave you, but always be led by the Holy Spirit and remember that "love never fails."

CHAPTER 7

The Practical Applications of Prayer

*I*n the chapter, "How to Pray for Various Conditions," you will see many references to the practical things you should do when praying for others. This chapter will explain these things.

Growing Out Legs

Chiropractors can often tell if a person has a back problem by measuring their legs. He asks the person to sit in a chair with their back firmly against the back of the chair. The chiropractor stands in front of the person holding their legs up with his thumbs on the sides of the anklebones and his hands over the top of the feet. Any difference in the leg length will be obvious by the displacement of his thumbs. They will not be adjacent to one another, indicating that one leg appears to be longer than the other.

I have yet to meet anyone with a serious back problem who had legs that measured the same length. This does not mean that the length of one leg is actually shorter than the other. (This only happens if there is bone loss from injury or a birth defect that left one leg shorter than the other. People with this condition will often be wearing a lift in their shoe to compensate for the short leg.) However, this does mean that the back is out of alignment. The spine, pelvis, muscles, tendons, or ligaments have moved to compensate for the problem, causing one leg to extend a shorter distance than the other. One leg appears to be shorter than the other.

I check the lengths of the legs in the same manner as a chiropractor. Following this example with your hands over their ankles and your thumbs on their ankle bones, command the back to line up.

Prayer to Adjust the Legs

"I command the brain stem and the spinal column to be in perfect alignment. I command the muscles, tendons, and ligaments to go back to their normal length and strength. I speak in new discs and vertebrae (when necessary). I command the pain to go and the legs to return to their normal position in Jesus' name."

Under no circumstances do you ever pull on the legs. Pray and wait until the ankles line up by the power of the Holy Spirit. Usually the legs will adjust quickly, but occasionally it may take several minutes.

Are there other ways to heal backs besides "growing out" legs? My answer is absolutely, "Yes." However, when you minister this way, you will see the power of God at work and so will the person for whom you are praying. Tell the person you are praying for, as well as anyone else watching nearby, to keep their eyes open and watch what God is doing. They don't want to miss their

51

miracle. Ministering healing this way for over thirty years, I have seen countless numbers of backs successfully healed by "growing out" legs.

Pelvis Adjustment

The pelvis is the foundation of the spine. If the back is out of alignment, the pelvis shifts in an attempt to keep the body as upright as possible. When the pelvis is out of alignment, it can cause numerous problems ranging from duck feet to PMS. To minister healing to an individual, simply place your hands loosely on the top of their hipbones. If you are ministering to someone of the opposite sex, instruct them to place their hands on their hipbones and then place your hands loosely over theirs. Repeat the prayer and then wait as the Holy Spirit does the adjustment. You may need to allow a few minutes for the adjustment to occur.

When you minister this way, you will see the power of God.

Prayer to Adjust the Pelvis

"I command the pelvis to rotate into its normal position. I command all the organs to go back into place and muscles, tendons, and ligaments to go back to their normal length and strength in Jesus' name."

Do not move the pelvis yourself. Wait on the Holy Spirit. What happens next is often astounding. The pelvis will often rotate back and forth and the people will many times feel their ligaments, organs, or pelvis move. When praying for a woman's PMS symptoms, command the ligaments to lengthen and the pelvis to open to alleviate pressure. For a quick and easy birth, command the pelvis to open for an easy delivery. If they have duck feet, command the pelvis to close. If they are pigeon-toed, command the pelvis to open.

Middle Back Adjustment

Through experience, I have found that many ailments caused by a curvature of the spine or pain in the region of the upper chest or back can be healed by commanding the ribs to rotate back into their normal position. I use this prayer when ministering healing to people with scoliosis and have seen many healed. Place your hand on the back of the spine in the center of the back and repeat this prayer:

Prayer for Adjustment of the Middle Back

"In the name of Jesus, I command the ribs to rotate and go back into place. I command the vertebrae and discs in the spine to line up. And I command all muscles, ligaments, and tendons to go back to their normal length and strength in Jesus' name."

Growing Out Arms

Chiropractors can often detect an upper back problem by measuring the length of the person's arms. With the individual standing, feet pointing forward, toes even, and arms extended straight forward to their fully outstretched length, the doctor instructs them to keep the hands about one quarter of an inch apart. When the arms are extended fully, the doctor tells the client to put their hands together, bend their elbows and look at the tips of their fingers. If the upper back is out of alignment, the position of the hands will not match.

It is not uncommon for someone with an upper back problem to have their arms appear to be different lengths. Unless there was a birth defect or bone loss at some time in their lives, the arms are not actually different lengths. Bones are positioned by ligaments, tendons, and muscles. Changes in their control affect the positioning and action of skeletal structures, our bones, including our arms, legs, back, pelvis, and neck.

I minister to people with upper back problems in the same way. Instruct the person to stand with their feet forward and stretch out their arms as far as they can with their hands facing each other about one quarter inch apart. Instruct them to put their hands together, bend their elbows, and look at the difference in their arm length. Instruct them to keep their eyes open to watch what God is going to do, to stretch out their arms again about one quarter inch apart, place your hand on the center of their upper back and repeat this prayer:

Prayer to Adjust Arm Length

"In the name of Jesus I command the upper back to go back into place and the brain stem to line up with the spinal column. I command the muscles, tendons, and ligaments to go back to their normal length and strength. I speak in a new disc and vertebra (if necessary). I also command the arms to grow and the pain to go in Jesus' name."

Under no circumstances do you ever push on the back or pull the arms. Pray and wait until the length of the arms line up by the power of the Holy Spirit. Usually, they will adjust quickly but occasionally the process may take several minutes.

Are there other ways to heal upper backs besides growing out arms? My answer is absolutely, "Yes." However, when you minister this way, you can watch the power of God at work. As long as the person that you are praying for keeps their eyes open, they will see as well as feel what God is doing. Anyone nearby can also see the changes as they occur. During the thirty years I have been ministering healing by growing out arms, I have seen countless upper back problems healed.

Adjusting the Neck

If the head or the neck is out of alignment, the muscles of the neck will tighten to compensate for the problem. This can be the cause of many problems from headaches to back spasms and even numbness in the extremities. Injuries caused by falls or whiplash can do major damage to the discs, vertebrae, muscles, tendons, and ligaments in the neck and upper back. To minister healing, stand in front of the person, place one hand on each side of the neck with your fingertips on the back of the neck directly over the spine and repeat the following prayer.

Prayer to Adjust the Neck and Spine

"In the name Jesus, I command the brain stem and the spinal column to come back into alignment. I command all the muscles, tendons, and ligaments to return to their normal length and strength. I speak in new discs and vertebrae (if necessary). I command the pain to go and the neck to go back into alignment in the name of Jesus."

Do not lift on the neck or turn it in any direction. After you have ministered, instruct them to turn their head and do something they could not comfortably do before.

Practical Things to Remember

1. You are ministering all healing in the name of Jesus. Always use His name with each command such as "I command (type of healing) in the name of Jesus."

2. After praying for someone, tell them to say, "Thank You, Jesus." Always thank Him first.

3. Next, have them put their faith into action. Instruct them to do something that they could not do before (especially if they had restricted movement).

4. If their symptoms are still present, pray again. Don't give up. Instruct them to expect their healing (the absence of symptoms, etc.) not the pain, while they are thanking God for the improvement and the eventual completion of the healing.

5. Never tell anyone to stop taking medication even when all the symptoms have disappeared. Tell them they must check with their doctors for instructions regarding any change in their medications.

6. A relationship with Jesus is what everyone needs most. If they are not born again, lead them in the prayer of salvation.

CHAPTER 8

God Gets the Glory

By this time you should be prepared to pray for people to be healed and blessed by God. It is not uncommon at the end of a ministry session for people who received healing to say, "Oh, thank you! Thank you!"

In return, most believers who are ministering will respond by saying, "Thank Jesus, not me," to turn the attention away from them and give the glory to God where it is due. Here is another way to deal with this same situation.

When people who were healed say, "Oh thank you! Thank you!" just respond by saying, "I just watched God answer your prayers. That's what happened here." That response removes you from the situation completely. It gives all the credit to God and makes you an observer of God's power rather than the source of that power. This will allow you to avoid that awkward moment when you have to deflect the glory from you to God. By telling them you watched God answer their prayers, you are saying God did it and He could have done it without you. It takes all the glory away from you and gives it to God where it belongs.

Wait on the Holy Spirit. He will move through you. It is not a function of your ability, but of your availability. The more mature you become in the Lord, the more you realize it never was by or through your ability that anyone was healed. Be aware of the words that come out of your mouth after you pray for someone. Are you rejoicing that they were touched and freed or are you talking about how you prayed for someone and how they got healed? Is it about you? Or is it about what God did for them?

After the fact, you can clearly see the motivation of your heart by the words that come out of your mouth. *"For out of the overflow of the heart the mouth speaks"* (Matthew 12:34). Your words will confirm whether your motivation is to see people set free or to elevate yourself by letting others know that when you pray for people, they are healed.

> *Wait on the Holy Spirit. He will move through you.*

It is not uncommon to be excited when someone is healed. I believe that you should be very excited. I get excited every time someone is healed. However, who gets the glory? Can you tell others about the healing without mentioning your participation in it at all? Is the ministry about you and your gifting or is it about God?

If you find that you have been self-centered in ministry, then this is the perfect time to repent. *"But if you harbor bitter envy and selfish ambition in your hearts, do not boast about it or deny the truth. Such 'wisdom' does not come down from heaven but is earthly, unspiritual, of the devil. For where you have envy and selfish ambition, there you find disorder and every evil practice"* (James 3:14–16).

If you have been selfish and your motives are for yourself, repent. Don't stop ministering to others, just do it with God's motives and not your own. It is not uncommon to meet powerfully gifted people who believe they are serving God with their gifts, but who may, in reality, be serving themselves. *"Many will say to me on that day, 'Lord, Lord, did we not prophesy in your name, and in your name drive out demons and perform many miracles?' Then I will tell them plainly, 'I never knew you. Away from me, you evildoers!'"* (Matthew 7:22–23).

Be sure to always give God all the glory.

CHAPTER 9

Ministry to Children

*W*hen you are ministering to children, always position yourself at eye level with them. Get on your knees or sit down in a chair. Always ask, "What is your name?" Don't talk about them or ask them personal questions when you first meet. Talk about your own children or some of your experiences as a child until they start to join in or until you know they are relaxed enough for you to minister to them.

Most children don't come running up to the front of the church for prayer. They are usually dragged to the altar by their parents. Parents often say things like, "Can you change this kid's habits and help them? We have tried everything." Or "He has had this medical problem or that problem since he was born." Take time to talk to the child on their level. Don't speak to them in baby talk, talk to them like an adult, because they are in front of an adult seeking help.

Take extra time if the child has not reached the age of accountability. The age of accountability is a Jewish custom that marks the time when children become (young) adults and they then stand before God responsible for their own actions. For a girl, the age of accountability begins when she starts menstruation (around twelve years of age) and for a boy, it begins when he can grow hair on his face (around the age of thirteen). These events essentially mean that they have entered puberty.

Mistakes prior to this age are not necessarily childish; however, responsibility for the consequences in Jewish law falls upon the parents, not the child. It is understood that the child may be fully aware of what they are doing and the consequences of their actions. Prior to this time or event, the child has not reached the age of accountability and is accountable only through the parents.

In many cases, I have found I do not need to pray for the child unless they specifically ask for prayer. I have found the greatest success by praying for the parents.

"For the unbelieving husband has been sanctified through his wife, and the unbelieving wife has been sanctified through her believing husband. Otherwise your children would be unclean, but as it is, they are holy" (1 Corinthians 7:14).

There is a Christian child psychologist in Florida who has had great success ministering to disturbed children with Attention Deficient Disorder (ADD) as well as other problems. He ministered only to the believing parents. Never once did he see the child. He met with the mom and dad, prayed with them, and instructed them on how to handle their child. Many times he would not only counsel them, but he would also give them homework assignments that had to be completed before he would meet with them again. All of the children changed in just a short period of time after he ministered only to the parents.

The sins of the fathers are carried down to the third and fourth generations. No one can avoid this spiritual law. Until someone repents (changes), this law remains in effect. The curse stops when somebody repents and stands in for his fathers and says, "No more, this sin stops here and now. I repent for my sins and the sins of my fathers."

When I was at a large church in Chicago, a mom started screaming in the back of the room. Running to the back, I found a young boy turning blue from a severe asthma attack. The parents had sent someone to the car to get his asthma medicine, but the church was packed and the car was parked a long distance from the church.

After asking the Lord what to do, I clearly heard Him say, "Pray for the mom." I took the hysterical mother to a quiet corner and led her in a prayer of repentance for adultery. She immediately repented and when she did, she felt something tangible leave her. At the same moment, the boy started breathing deeply. He was fine. The mother's repentance and the boy's recovery happened simultaneously. I never touched the boy or laid hands on him, yet he was healed.

I am not telling you that asthma is caused by adultery, but rather that it is caused by the sins of the fathers (a parent or an ancestor). In this case, there was a particular situation involving sin. The asthma and this sinful situation started at the same time and repentance brought healing to both at the same time.

The Bible has a great deal to say about the effects of the sins of the fathers (Exodus 34:5–7; Leviticus 26:39–42; Numbers 14:18).

"You shall not bow down to them or worship them; for I, the Lord your God, am a jealous God, punishing the children for the sin of the fathers to the third and fourth generation of those who hate me" (Exodus 20:5).

Jesus also spoke about the sins of the fathers. He told the Pharisees that they were doing the same things their fathers did.

"Abraham is our father," they answered. "If you were Abraham's children," said Jesus, "then you would do the things Abraham did. As it is, you are determined to kill me, a man who has told you the truth that I heard from God. Abraham did not do such things. You are doing the things your own father does." (John 8:39–41)

When you lead people in prayers of repentance, it is important to have them repent for the sins of their fathers (parents, grandparents, ancestors) as well. Then tell them to put all these sins on the cross of Jesus Christ. (See Chapter 11 for specific prayers.)

*M*inistering deliverance is not complicated or difficult. It is as easy as praying for the sick. It does, however, require an understanding of God's Word and a comprehension of God's authority. Deliverance was one-third of Jesus' ministry. If you are going to lay hands on the sick and see them recover, it will also be a part of your ministry.

What is a demonic being? It is an evil spirit that is looking for a body to inhabit and needs a doorway in which to enter. Can Christians have demons? My answer is always the same: Do Christians have bodies? Remember that the cause of sickness is sin and sin is also the doorway that many demonic spirits use to move into a person's life. Demons can't inhabit your spirit; but given the right into your life, they can affect your body and your soul, which is your mind, your will, and your emotions. You will not find demons behind every doorknob or rose bush, but they do exist and they can reap havoc on God's people.

If you are not familiar with the Scriptures that show that demons exist and how they operate, you need to read and reread them again. Begin with the healing ministry of Jesus. Jesus cast seven demons out of Mary Magdalene and went on to cast demons out of many others also (Mark 16:9; Matthew 8:16, 28–32; 10:8, Mark 1:32–34, 39; Luke 8:2; 27–33;11:14 as well as many other Scripture verses).

Demons (or devils) are not the cause of every problem in life. However, if they are the cause of the problem in the person coming to you for ministry, you need to know how to minister deliverance (freedom) according to God's Word.

How do I deal with these spirit entities? First of all, you need to know you have authority over demons. This authority is given by God to all believers without exception. *"And these signs will accompany those who believe: In my name they will drive out demons"* (Mark 16:17). He gave us this authority, just as He gave it to His disciples. He called His twelve disciples to Him and gave them authority to drive out evil spirits and to heal every disease

> *You have the authority given by God to all believers.*

and sickness. Jesus gave His followers the authority to deliver others from demons. If you are a follower of Jesus, then you have the same authority (Matthew 10:1; Mark 3:14–15; 6:7–13; 16:17; Luke 9:1; 10:17–19). It is interesting to consider that His followers ministered healing and cast out demons both before and after Jesus died as well as before and after they received the Holy Spirit in the book of Acts.

Along with being fully persuaded that you have this authority, you must also have an understanding of how it functions. This authority is yours when you understand your position in Christ and not just your power or abilities in Him. It may be best explained this way: You are driving down the highway at night and a big man on a large motorcycle tries to get you to pull off the road. There is no doubt you would resist him. However, if a police officer on a patrol motorcycle tries to pull you over, you know you have stop. He is no stronger than the other man but he is operating within a higher authority and counts on that power to back him up. He knows and understands his authority.

It is not what you can do to the demons that gets them to obey, but it is who you are in Christ that they have to submit to. *"The seventy-two returned with joy and said, 'Lord, even the demons submit to us in your name'"* (Luke 10:17).

How do you know which demons or evil spirits are causing a problem? In general, they are described by their function, meaning how these spiritual beings manifest in the natural realm. The Word of God mentions many types such as a spirit of infirmity (Luke 7:21; 8:2; 13:11 KJV), deaf and dumb spirits (Mark 7:32, 37; 9:25), the spirit of heaviness (Isaiah 61:3 KJV), the spirit of haughtiness or pride (Proverbs 16:18), a spirit of bondage (Romans 8:15 KJV) etc.

I have found through life experiences that demons are singular in their purpose. There are many types of evil spirits or demons and each one has its own manifestation. For example, a spirit of anger can only manifest as anger. A spirit of infirmity can only manifest as sickness. And a spirit of perversion is always perverse and has no other traits.

Setting people free from demons is very easy because demons must obey believers acting under the authority of God using the name of Jesus. However, there is this one caution: as in any ministry, make sure you are led by the Spirit and not by your own desires to see someone set free. Jesus clearly explained that if I cast a spirit out of someone but neglect to deal with the cause (doorway) in which the spirit came in, I could be doing more harm than good.

> *When an evil spirit comes out of a man, it goes through arid places seeking rest and does not find it. Then it says, "I will return to the house I left." When it arrives, it finds the house swept clean and put in order. Then it goes and takes seven other spirits more wicked than itself, and they go in and live there. And the final condition of that man is worse than the first.* (Luke 11:24–26)

It is very important that the root cause is dealt with and that there is repentance from this cause. There are two very important questions to ask in order to find the root cause:

1. How long have you had the problem? (When did it start?)

2. What happened just before or when the problem started? (Identify the doorway.)

Fear, unforgiveness, bitterness, pride, lust, greed, generational sins, curses, and any participation in the occult are just a few of the root causes.

A woman in Iowa had been in pain for four years. She had been in an auto accident and her back had never healed even though she had often received prayer. There had been an ugly insurance lawsuit and she had been falsely accused. She was still angry with both the person who hit her and their attorney. When I prayed for her, she forgave them both and was instantly healed. As she forgave them, she could feel the anger, bitterness, and pain leave her body.

I could have ministered to her by just casting out the spirit of pain. However, if I had not led her in repentance for the anger and unforgiveness, she may have had even more problems if the spirit of pain returned (Luke 11:24–26).

Setting people free is easy. When you are ministering, don't look for the darkness that may be residing in people. Look for the light that is in them and the light will expose any darkness. I also want to point out that there is no record in the Bible where Jesus ever yelled at the demons or repeated Himself over and over again. He simply drove them out with a word. *"When evening came, many who were demon-possessed were brought to him, and he drove out the spirits with a word and healed all the sick"* (Matthew 8:16).

Also, you must remember that when the demons are driven out, they can't go into you, your family members, or even your house. The word confirms that they go to the dry and arid places. *"When an evil spirit comes out of a man, it goes through arid places seeking rest and does not find it"* (Luke 11:24). The dry and arid places are places without the water of life (Revelation 22:1).

> *Always walk according to God's truth as revealed in His Word.*

Although evil spirits still exist, are still evil, and still have power, always remember they all have to submit to the name that is above every name, the name of Jesus Christ. *"At the name of Jesus every knee should bow, in heaven and on earth and under the earth"* (Philippians 2:10).

The demons do not have to submit to your will, but they have to submit to God's will through the name of Jesus. So, always walk according to God's truth as revealed in His Word, be led by the peace of God, and follow the leading of the Holy Spirit.

Prayers of Repentance

his is a collection of effective prayers that you will use in the "How to Pray for Various Conditions" section of this book. They are very effective in ministering healing. Learn them.

Prayer of Salvation

"Father, I know that Jesus came that we may have life and that life more abundantly (John 10:10). The Word of God confirms that he who follows Jesus must be a servant of the Lord. As that servant, he would lose the life he knows and would receive a new life in Christ (Mark 10:43; Romans 6:4). I am willing to die to my old life and pick up this new life as a servant of the Lord Jesus Christ.

"Father, I confess I have been living for myself. The path I have chosen has not produced life-giving fruit that lasts. I am willing to give my whole life to You and confess with my mouth that Jesus is Lord and that I am now the servant of the Lord. No longer will I live for myself, but I will live for Christ from this day forth. I confess my sins and ask that they be removed from me and put on the cross of Jesus Christ. (Take the time needed to confess these sins.) I know this is the beginning of a journey that will continue through eternity. I (insert full Christian name) give you 100 percent of my heart and confirm my covenant with Jesus who is raised from the dead and now lives in my heart."

Prayer for Forgiveness

"Father, I understand that You do not forgive sin but You do forgive people who sin (Matthew 6:12). I understand that You separate the sins from those who confess and repent of those sins. The Word of God confirms that Jesus bore my confessed sins on the cross and that He no longer holds them against me (1 Peter 2:24). I also understand that no one but Jesus deserved forgiveness and that You will forgive me of my sins with the same measure that I choose to forgive others (Matthew 6:14–15).

"Father, I choose to forgive (insert name). What they did to me is sin. Take this sin from them and put it on the cross. And on the day of judgment when I stand before Your Throne, I will hold no accusation against them. Father, I ask you to bless them, in Jesus' name."

Repentance for Judgment and Condemnation

"Father, I understand Your Word says You will judge me with the same measure I use to judge others. I also know by Your Word that I will be condemned with the same measure that I use to condemn others (Luke 6:37–38; 1 Corinthians 5:12). I know it is correct to judge things as right and wrong according to your Word, but only You know the motives and intent of another's heart (Hebrews 4:12).

"Father, I have judged others and condemned them. This is sin, and I repent of this sin and ask You to separate this sin from me in Jesus' name and put it on the cross of Jesus Christ."

Prayer to Break Word Curses

"Father, I know Your Word says to say things that edify, build up, correct in love, and confirm (1 Thessalonians 5:11; 2 Timothy 4:2). Words of condemnation, slander, complaining, griping, and gossip or accusation are not of You. They are sin (James 5:9).

"Father, I have said words that did not edify, exhort, correct in love, or confirm. I take responsibility for those words. They are sin. Take this sin from me, put it on the cross of Jesus, and on the day of judgment, hold no accusations against me. I renounce those words in Jesus' name. I ask you to bless those whom I have said bad words about.

"Father, people have said words about me that did not edify, exhort, correct in love or confirm. That is sin. Take the sin from them, put it on the cross of Jesus and on the day of judgment, hold no accusations against them. They are free. I choose to release them from this, and those words are now broken off me, in Jesus' name."

Prayer to Break Generational Curses

"Father, I know Your Word says that if we confess our iniquity (sins) and the iniquity (sins) of our fathers that you will heal us (James 5:16; Leviticus 26:40–42).

"Father, I take responsibility for my sins. I ask You to forgive me of my sins, separate them from me, and place them on the cross of Jesus Christ. I also ask you to forgive my fathers of this same sin, separate their sins from them, put them on the cross as well and thus break the curse off of me and my family, in Jesus' name."

Prayer to Break Ungodly Covenants

"Father, I understand that sexual intercourse is the sign of the marriage covenant and that you call the marriage covenant holy (Matthew 19:6). I know Your Word states that sex outside of marriage is sin (Matthew 15:19–20). I also understand that I have entered into covenant with every person with whom I have had sexual relations.

"Father, I renounce the ungodly covenant I made with (insert name). This was sin and I renounce it as such. Separate this sin from me, place it on the cross of Jesus, and break this covenant I made off of me and my household. I also renounce any other ungodly covenants I have made as well, in Jesus' name."

CHAPTER 12

The Immune System and Electrical and Magnetic Frequencies, Prions, and pH Balance

*T*he immune system consists of a group of highly special-ized interactive cells, which recognize abnormal cells, tissues, objects, or organisms within the body or that enter the body. When the abnormality is identified, the immune response is initiated. The white blood cells within the lymph fluid then attack the abnormalities to destroy them, remove them from the body, and return the body to its normal healthy state.

Lymph tissues are found in many areas throughout the body such as the bone marrow, tonsils, adenoids, spleen, and appendix. These organs and tissues act as a protective network of barriers to infection and/or foreign bodies. The lymph vessels and lymph nodes are parts of the special circulatory system that carry lymph throughout the body and are vital to the immune response.

Although their systems are completely separate, the lymph and blood circulatory systems work in close partnership with each other to clear impurities from the body such as bacteria, infection, viruses, or cancer cells.

God designed other specific protective barriers within the body also. These include the skin (the largest organ of the body), stomach acid, mucous, cough reflex, tears, and skin oils. If a foreign organism gets past these lines of defense, the immune system takes over to fight off the potentially dangerous substance.

Most diseases start when the immune system is compromised. Add this command wherever applicable:

Prayer to Restore the Immune System

"I command the immune system to be restored. I command it to be effective in stopping diseases, germs, and viruses from inflicting this body, in Jesus' name."

Electrical and Magnetic Frequencies

The human body is made up of trillions of cells that are affected by constant chemical reactions, which produce energy for our life functions. Part of the energy released from these reactions is electrical energy that has its own magnetic frequency. Modern science is now able to measure these electrical and magnetic frequencies.

Science has found that in bodies where sickness such as cancer exists, the electrical and magnetic frequencies are altered from their natural state. In other words, these frequencies are out of harmony and balance. There are studies that suggest that cancer ceases to grow when the electrical and magnetic frequencies are returned to their natural state. I have found by my own experiences that commanding the body to return to its natural electrical and magnetic frequencies has brought healing with many diseases.

Prayer to Normalize Electrical and Magnetic Frequencies

"In the name of Jesus I command all of the electrical and magnetic frequencies in this body to return to normal harmony and balance."

Prions

Prions are molecules of a normal body protein that have changed their normal configuration. They are capable of reproduction on their own and can become infectious, damage the body and negatively affect normal body function. These prions have been found in neurological tissues such as the brain on autopsy. Medical research is unclear as to the exact cause of prions as well as the treatment to control or prevent prion development. However, prions tend to exist where disease is present.

I have seen people healed of various diseases by simply commanding the prions to dissolve and be discarded by the body.

Prayer to Remove Prions

"I command all the prions to completely dissolve and be discarded from the body. I command healing to every cell affected by these prions, in Jesus' name."

pH Balance

The pH balance (acid/alkaline measurement) of our body fluids affects every cell in our bodies. Any imbalance will interfere with cellular activities and functions. Generalized complaints of low energy, fatigue, excess weight, poor digestion, headaches and other pains, as well as other more serious disorders have been connected to a pH imbalance. The causes often are from poor diet, drug toxicity, kidney or liver malfunction, breathing problems and/or uncontrolled diabetic management.

The body has many ways to correct any abnormal state or function of the body; however, it cannot correct all imbalanced states indefinitely. Certain diseases of the body can cause the pH imbalance; however, the imbalance itself will eventually cause other malfunctions or diseases of the body also. If not corrected, pH imbalance can cause death.

Prayer to Normalize the pH Balance

"I command the pH balance of this body to normalize. I command healing to every cell affected by any abnormal pH levels, in Jesus' name."

CHAPTER 13

Prayers for Various Conditions

ABUSE

Abuse may occur in the form of physical, sexual, emotional, verbal, or a combination of any of these and may be experienced at any age. If a responsible person does not provide the basic needs for a helpless, dependent person, the neglect is considered abuse as well. By law, we are required to report any ongoing sexual abuse of a minor. If you have been informed of such abuse and don't report it to the proper authorities, you can be prosecuted as well as the person who committed the crime. Victims often believe that they are responsible for the abusive treatment. They believe a lie.

How to Minister: (All commands done in Jesus' name.)

1. Instruct victims of ongoing physical abuse to go to a safe house.
2. Lead them in the prayer of forgiveness towards the abuser.
3. Rebuke the lies they have believed.
4. Speak the peace of God upon them.

ACNE

Acne is a skin condition characterized by whiteheads, blackheads, and inflamed red pimples or "zits." Acne is caused when the tiny pores on the surface of the skin become clogged. Normally, the oil glands beneath the skin surface help keep the skin lubricated and help remove old skin cells. When too much oil is produced, the pores can become blocked trapping dirt, debris, and bacteria. The bacteria can become infection that, in turn, can cause repeated skin eruptions that can leave serious physical scarring. Usually seen on the face, Acne can also affect other areas of the body such as the back.

Acne can be exacerbated by stress, incorrect diet, or poor hygiene. The unpleasant appearance of eruptions often affects relationships and can precipitate name-calling or isolation, especially in the formative teen years.

How to Minister: (All commands done in Jesus' name.)

1. Rebuke the infection and command it to go.
2. Lay hands on their head, commanding the skin pores to open, drain, and function normally.
3. Command glands to produce a normal amount of oil.
4. Command all damaged and scarred tissues be healed.
5. Speak peace to them.

ADDICTION (ALCOHOL, CIGARETTE, DRUGS, OR FOOD)

An Addiction is a physical and/or psychological dependence on a substance. For example: alcohol, nicotine in cigarettes, or drugs (such as tranquilizers, cocaine, marijuana, heroin etc.). Chronic abuse of any kind of drugs can cause damage to various organs and functions of the body. People can also be addicted to eating food (called Gluttony).

The root cause is most often rebellion that generally occurs at or just after puberty (the age of accountability) and opens the door to an addictive spirit. Many are able to get free of substance abuse but must fight with the addictive spirit their entire life until they repent of their rebellion.

How to Minister: (All commands done in Jesus' name.)

1. Confirm their desire to be free from the addiction.
2. Have them repent for their rebellion.
3. Have them renounce the words spoken in rebellion.
4. Speak a replacement for any damaged parts of their body, for example a new brain, liver, etc.
5. Speak peace to them.

ADDISON'S DISEASE (ALSO CALLED ADRENAL INSUFFICIENCY. SEE ADRENAL GLANDS ALSO.)

Addison's Disease is an endocrine or hormonal disorder. The disease is characterized by weight loss, muscle weakness, fatigue, low blood pressure, and sometimes an abnormal darkening of the skin.

Addison's Disease occurs when the adrenal glands do not produce enough hormones. Also called Adrenal Insufficiency, Addison's Disease may be due to a genetic abnormality of the adrenal glands. However, most cases are caused by the gradual destruction of the adrenal glands by the body's own immune system. (See Chapter 12 for additional information about the immune system and autoimmune disorders.)

How to Minister: (All commands done in Jesus' name.)

1. Lead them in the prayer of repentance for the sins of their fathers.
2. Command the electrical frequencies and chemical balance to be in order.

79

3. Command a creative miracle—a new pair of Adrenal Glands.
4. Command the hormones from the Adrenal Gland to maintain normal levels.

ADHESIONS (See Scars, Keloids, and Adhesions.)

ADRENAL GLANDS (Also see Addison's Disease.)

The Adrenal Glands are located on top of both kidneys. These glands secrete hormones such as adrenaline that affect blood pressure, heart rate, and sweating. In times of tension or anxiety, the Adrenal Glands put out extra adrenaline so the body can adequately cope with the "stress." It secretes many hormones that control the use of fats, proteins, and carbohydrates in the body, as well as male sex hormones. The glands also secrete a mineral corticoid that controls blood pressure and the levels of salt and potassium in the body.

The hypothalamus or pituitary glands produce other hormones that, in turn, control the Adrenal Glands. Abnormal functioning of these other glands can cause problems with the Adrenal Glands. Abnormal production of hormones, disease, or infection inside or immediately around the Adrenal Glands can cause problems as well.

People with a disorder of the Adrenal Glands are often stressed constantly, worried or overworked, and take little time to adequately rest or sleep.

How to Minister: (All commands done in Jesus' name.)

1. Rebuke any infection or underlying disease process and command the Adrenal Glands to function properly.
2. Command all hormones to return to normal levels.

3. Lead in a prayer of repentance for worry (lay worry on the altar of God), stress (give problems to Jesus) or not resting (God requires a Sabbath day's rest).

ADRENAL INSUFFICIENCY (See Addison's Disease.)

AGORAPHOBIA (See Panic Disorder.)

AIDS/HIV

HIV (Human Immunodeficiency Virus) is the virus that causes AIDS (Acquired Immunodeficiency Syndrome). This virus may be passed from one person to another through infected blood, semen, or vaginal secretions when they come in contact with an uninfected person's broken skin or mucous membranes (mouth, eyes, nose, vagina, rectum, or opening of the penis). In addition, infected pregnant women can pass HIV to their baby during pregnancy or delivery as well as through breast-feeding. It can also be passed by sharing infected needles or through blood transfusions.

People with HIV have the HIV infection. Some of these people will develop AIDS while others won't. AIDS is an acronym for Acquired Immunodeficiency Syndrome. *Acquired* means that the disease developed after birth from contact with a disease (in this case, HIV). *Immunodeficiency* means that the disease is characterized by a weakening of the immune system. *Syndrome* refers to a number of symptoms that indicate or characterize a disease when they occur simultaneously. In the case of AIDS, the syndrome includes the development of certain infections and/or cancers, as well as an abnormality in the number of certain cells in the infected person's immune system.

How to Minister: (All commands done in Jesus' name.)

1. Lead in repentance when necessary.
2. Rebuke the spirit of HIV.

3. Speak in a new immune and blood system.
4. Command the electrical and magnetic frequencies to be in harmony and return to normal balance.
5. Command all prions to completely dissolve and leave the body.
6. Command the blood to come into proper pH balance.
7. Command all damaged organs and tissues to return to normal function and appearance.

ALLERGIES

Allergic reactions are the body's inappropriate immune response to normally harmless substances, which are often environmental. The immune system defends the body against foreign substances. However, in susceptible people, the immune system can overreact to certain substances that are harmless to most people. The result is an allergic reaction.

About one third of the people in the United States have some type of allergy. Allergic reactions can occur when the substance lands on the skin or in the eye, is inhaled, eaten, or injected. A seasonal Allergy (such as hay fever) is caused by exposure to airborne particles from such sources as grass or ragweed pollen or perfume. An allergic reaction can be caused by a medication, eating certain foods, breathing in dust, smoke, animal dander, changes in physical conditions such as walking into a cold room or bright light, or touching an object e.g. cosmetics or soaps.

Reactions can manifest by a slightly runny nose, mild itching, or headache; or the effects can be life threatening with severe breathing difficulties that, if not treated immediately, can lead to death.

How to Minister: (All commands done in Jesus' name.)

1. Lead them in a prayer of repentance for generational curses.

2. Lay hands on the head, commanding the immune system to return to normal, and all the tissues and organs to be healed and function normally.
3. If not an inherited trait, find out what happened just before symptoms began and lead in a prayer for repentance or forgiveness.

ALOPECIA (See Baldness.)

ALZHEIMER'S DISEASE

Alzheimer's Disease is characterized by a progressive loss of mental function. Parts of the brain degenerate and destroyed nerve cells can no longer transmit signals from the brain to the body. Mentation diminishes to some degree in all people as they age but is much more pronounced in those affected by Alzheimer's.

This severely debilitating condition can lead to the person's total dependence for all activities of daily living and requires constant supervision. The total disorientation, personality changes, abnormal behavior, and loss of memory affect the person as well as the entire family.

The cause of Alzheimer's is unknown, but the disease seems to occur more frequently in some families. In the United States, millions of people have been diagnosed with Alzheimer's Disease. Elevated concentrations of aluminum have been found in the brain of some people while other patients have been misdiagnosed and found to have excessive spinal fluid that exerts pressure on the brain causing symptoms similar to Alzheimer's Disease.

How to Minister: (All commands done in Jesus' name.)

1. Lead them in a prayer of repentance for generational curses.
2. Command the metallic levels in the blood and the brain to return to normal.
3. Command the excessive spinal fluid to return to normal.

4. Speak a creative miracle and command a new brain.
5. Command all nerve pathways and communication between the brain and body to return to normal.

AMBLYOPIA (ALSO CALLED LAZY EYE.)

Amblyopia is loss of vision in one eye. This usually can be traced to a lack of use of that eye in early childhood. This type of vision loss is usually caused by the abnormal functioning of the brain, not of the eye. Amblyopia is the most common cause of vision loss in children and develops only during childhood. Amblyopia should be suspected if the eyes turn inward or outward, the eyes do not appear to work together or if the person shows a lack of depth perception.

Crossed eyes, farsightedness, nearsightedness, astigmatism, and childhood cataracts are common causes of Amblyopia. As one eye becomes dominant and has normal vision, images from the weaker eye are ignored by the brain and the visual system in the brain fails to develop properly. Between ages 5 and 10, the condition becomes permanent.

How to Minister: (All commands done in Jesus' name.)

1. Command the eyes to send complete signals to the brain.
2. Command the brain to interpret the messages from both eyes and function normally.
3. Command the eye muscles to be of equal length and strength and the nerves to function normally.
4. Command the eye to be healed and vision to be normal.
5. Lead them in a prayer of repentance for generational curses.

AMYOTROPHIC LATERAL SCLEROSIS (ALS)

Also known as "Lou Gehrig's disease" or "ALS," Amyotrophic Lateral Sclerosis is characterized by progressive loss of motor nerve function in the spinal cord and brain. Motor nerves control the voluntary movement of muscles. Some cases of ALS have been linked to a genetic defect while, in many other cases, the cause of the nerve deterioration is unknown. It eventually can lead to paralysis of the respiratory system and dependency upon mechanical ventilators to maintain life.

How to Minister: (All commands done in Jesus' name.)

1. Lead them in a prayer of repentance for generational curses.
2. Command the spirit of ALS to leave.
3. Command a new nervous system and a new brain.
4. Command that all systems be totally healed and function normally.

ANEMIA (SEE ALSO SICKLE CELL ANEMIA.)

Red blood cells contain hemoglobin, a protein that enables the cells to carry oxygen from the lungs and to all parts of the body. When the number of red blood cells is reduced or the amount of hemoglobin is low, the blood cannot supply sufficient oxygen to the cells of the body. Without enough oxygen, the organs of the body do not function effectively and the symptoms of Anemia appear—extreme weakness, shortness of breath with any exertion, pale lips, skin, and nail beds, to name a few.

Anemia can be caused by a lack of vitamin B-12 that is essential for normal nervous system function and blood cell production. The main dietary sources of vitamin B-12 include meat, eggs, and dairy products. Anemia can also be caused by a slow loss of blood within the body such as a bleeding ulcer in the GI tract, irritable bowel syndrome, or cancer. Because red blood cells are produced in the bone marrow, any problems or malfunction of the bone marrow can also cause Anemia.

How to Minister: (All commands done in Jesus' name.)

1. Command the gastrointestinal tract to be healed and to properly absorb and utilize necessary vitamins and minerals, especially Vitamin B-12.
2. Command the bone marrow to function normally and to manufacture normal amounts of healthy red blood cells.
3. Command any source of abnormal bleeding to be healed and function normally.
4. Command the blood to come into proper pH balance.

ANEURYSM

An Aneurysm is a bulge (dilated weak section) in the wall of an artery, usually the aorta (the large blood vessel leading from the heart to the body); however, an Aneurysm can develop in other arteries of the body as well, such as within the brain. The pressure of blood inside an artery forces a weakened area to balloon outward. If untreated, an Aneurysm may rupture, resulting in serious internal bleeding. If the rupture is in the brain, serious brain damage or death can occur. If located in or near the heart, death occurs rapidly.

The most common cause of an aortic Aneurysm is atherosclerosis, which weakens the wall of the aorta. Less common causes include injuries, inflammatory diseases of the blood vessel, and some infectious diseases such as syphilis. In older people, almost all Aneurysms are associated with atherosclerosis. High blood pressure, common among older people, and cigarette smoking both increase the risk of an Aneurysm.

How to Minister: (All commands done in Jesus' name.)

1. Lay hands on the affected area, commanding a creative miracle—new arteries with good strong walls.
2. Command restoration of normal blood flow.

ANGINA

Angina is chest pain caused by inadequate blood flow through the blood vessels of the heart muscle. Angina is not a heart attack, but may be a symptom of heart disease and, if untreated, can lead to a heart attack. The decreased blood flow actually causes a type of "cramp" of the heart muscle. If the blood is cut off or diminished for an extended period, the cells of the heart muscle will die. At that point, the diagnosis will be a heart attack.

Inadequate blood supply to the heart can be and often is caused by atherosclerosis (thickening of the inside walls of the blood vessels).

How to Minister: (All commands done in Jesus' name.)

1. Command the blood vessels around the heart to open up completely and allow sufficient blood flow to the heart muscle.
2. Speak in a new heart.

ANOREXIA NERVOSA

A person with Anorexia Nervosa has a distorted body image, an extreme fear of obesity, refuses to maintain minimal normal body weight, and, in women, does not have menstrual periods. Hereditary factors may play a role in the development of Anorexia Nervosa, although social factors are also important. The desire to be thin pervades Western society, and a person who is obese is considered unattractive, unhealthy, and undesirable.

Children are aware of these attitudes at a young age. Two thirds of all adolescent girls from age twelve to eighteen will diet or use other extreme measures to control their weight. Occasionally, it is found in adults. The primary cause appears to be rebellion as stated in the Psalms. This generally starts with words of rebellion stated during or right after puberty.

"Some became fools through their rebellious ways and suffered affliction because of their iniquities. They loathed all food and drew near the gates of death" (Psalms 107:17–18).

How to Minister: (All commands done in Jesus' name.)

1. Have them repent of their rebellion at adolescence.
2. Have them renounce the words spoken in rebellion.
3. Cast out the spirit of death and speak in life.

ANXIETY (SEE ALSO FEAR AND PANIC DISORDER.)

Anxiety includes feeling apprehension, fear, or uneasiness. The source is not always known or recognized, which can add to the distress a person feels. The most effective solution is to identify and address the source of the stress, fear, or anxiety. Unfortunately, this is not always possible. Ask what the person thinks might be making them "stress out." Is something constantly on their mind? What do they worry about most? Does anything in particular make them sad or depressed? Talking with a friend or family member may be helpful with identifying the causative incident or triggering events.

How to Minister: (All commands done in Jesus' name.)

1. Lead them in a prayer to lay all worry, stress, and care on the altar of God.
2. Lead them in a prayer of repentance when necessary.
3. Speak peace to them.

APPESTAT (SEE OBESITY)

The Appestat is the brain's control center for the appetite (or desire for food).

ARMS AND HANDS

Numbness, tingling, and pain of the arms and hands are usually caused by a neck problem that affects the nerves and sensations to these areas. Increased tension, injury, and damage to the nerves, muscles, and spine can contribute to problems of the upper extremities.

How to Minister: (All commands done in Jesus' name.)

1. Grow out the arms.
2. Command the neck to be adjusted.
3. Command the nerves to be restored to normal structure and function.
4. Command numbness, tingling, and pain to go
5. Lead them in a prayer to lay all worry, stress and care on the altar of God.

ARTERIOSCLEROSIS (ALSO CALLED ATHEROSCLEROSIS.)

Arteriosclerosis is a condition in which patchy deposits of fatty material develop in the walls of medium and large-sized arteries, leading to reduced or blocked blood flow to tissues or organs of the body. Blockage of blood can permanently damage tissues and their function. Within the heart, blockage results in a heart attack, which can be life threatening. Blockage in the brain can cause a stroke, paralysis, or death.

Atherosclerosis can affect the arteries of the brain, heart, kidneys, other vital organs, and legs. It is the most important and most common type of Arteriosclerosis, a general term for several diseases in which the artery wall thickens and becomes less elastic because of the fat deposits.

How to Minister: (All commands done in Jesus' name.)

1. Command the neck to be adjusted.
2. Command all the arteries to be cleansed of all cholesterol deposits and elasticity to return to normal.

3. Command all blockages to disappear and blood to flow to every area of the body normally.
4. Command any damaged tissues or organs be healed and function normally.

ARTHRITIS (ALSO SEE OSTEOARTHRITIS AND RHEUMATOID ARTHRITIS)

Arthritis involves inflammation of one or more joints and the breakdown of the joint cartilage, which normally protects the joints and allows smooth movement. Cartilage also absorbs shock when pressure is placed on the joint as a person walks or it otherwise bears weight. Without the usual amount of cartilage, the bones rub together, causing pain, swelling, and stiffness in hips, knees, or feet. It can develop in any joint of the body including the hands, arms, shoulders, neck, and back.

How to Minister: (All commands done in Jesus' name.)
1. Cast out the spirit of Arthritis.
2. Command all inflammation and swelling to be healed and pain to go.
3. Command the cartilage to be restored and joints to function normally.
4. Lead in the prayer of forgiveness.

ASTHMA (ALSO SEE COPD.)

Asthma is a disease in which inflammation of the body's airways restricts airflow into and out of the lungs. When an Asthma attack occurs, the muscles of the airways tighten and the lining of the airways swell, reducing airflow and producing a characteristic wheezing sound. Increased mucus production also blocks the airways. Most people with Asthma have intermittent attacks, but can experience chronic mild shortness of breath with occasional episodes of increased breathing difficulty. Asthma attacks can last from minutes to days, and can become life-threatening if breathing is severely restricted by the swelling of tissues or blocked by excessive mucous production. Quite often, panic occurs at the same time, which can exacerbate the attack.

How to Minister: (All commands done in Jesus' name.)

1. Lead in repentance for the sins of the fathers.
2. Cast out the spirit of Asthma.
3. Speak healing to all the tissues of the respiratory system, all damage to other parts of the body be repaired, and all function be normal.
4. Grow out the arms.
5. Speak the peace of God into their life.

ASTIGMATISM

Astigmatism is a common condition of the eye. The cornea of the eye is not evenly curved and causes vision to be out of focus. The cause is unknown but it is usually present from birth and often occurs together with nearsightedness or farsightedness. A small amount of Astigmatism is normal and can be corrected with glasses.

How to Minister: (All commands done in Jesus' name.)

1. Command the spirit of astigmatism to go.
2. Command the eye(s) to return to the proper shape and vision to return to normal.

ATTENTION DEFICIT DISORDER (ADD)/ ATTENTION DEFICIT HYPERACTIVITY DISORDER (ADHD)

ADD and ADHD both include problems with attentiveness, hyperactivity, impulsive behavior, or any combination of these behaviors. ADHD affects school performance as well as development of relationships with others. Parents of children with ADHD are often exhausted, frustrated, and overwhelmed.

Diagnosed more often in boys than in girls, Attention Deficit Disorder (ADD) is the most commonly diagnosed behavioral disorder of childhood. Every child suspected of having ADHD or ADD needs a careful professional evaluation to determine what is contributing to the abnormal behaviors. Symptoms such as depression, sleep deprivation, learning disabilities, tic disorders, and behavior problems may be confused with, or appear along with, ADHD.

How to Minister: (All commands done in Jesus' name.)

1. Lead them in a prayer of repentance for the sins of the fathers.
2. Command silence to all the abnormal noises in the head.
3. Command the spirit of ADD/ADHD to go.
4. Speak in a new brain, if necessary.
5. Command the hormones to be in balance and the nerve pathways of the brain to work properly
6. Command peace to the family and the home.
7. Suggest a change in diet where applicable.

AUTISM

Autism is a complex developmental disorder that appears in the first years of life, although it can sometimes be diagnosed much later. Affecting the brain's normal development of communication and social skills, it encompasses a wide range of behavior. The common features of Autism include impaired social interactions, impaired verbal and nonverbal communication, and restricted and repetitive patterns of behavior.

How to Minister: (All commands done in Jesus' name.)

1. Gently and with a quiet attitude, hold the person if possible.
2. Speaking softly but firmly, command the spirit of Autism to go.
3. Lay on hands and command a new brain and the total restoration of the nervous system.
4. Speak the peace of God into their heart and soul.

BACK PROBLEMS (ALSO SEE DISC PROBLEMS.)

Back pain is one of the most common complaints treated by physicians. Nearly four out of five people will experience back pain at some time in their lives. The vast majority of these cases do not have a specific identifiable cause for the pain.

Back pain can develop from such things as muscle strain, injury, overuse, muscle disorders, pressure on a nerve root, poor posture, ruptured discs, or spinal fractures. Pregnant women, smokers, construction workers, and people who perform repetitive lifting are at increased risk for back problems, which can result in chronic pain.

How to Minister: (All commands done in Jesus' name.)

Pinpoint the problem when possible. (For example, ask: What is the doctor's diagnosis? What do you know specifically about the problem? Do you have pain? Were you in an accident? Have you had surgery?)

1. For lower back problems, grow out the legs.
2. For pain of the middle back, grow out the arms.
3. For upper back pain, command the neck to come into proper alignment.
4. Command the pelvis to rotate into the perfect position for the spine to line up perfectly.

93

5. Do any or all of these as needed and repeat, if necessary.
6. Command the discs, vertebrae, muscles, ligaments, and tendons to be healed and adjusted. Be specific when possible.
7. Speak a new disc or vertebrae into the back, if necessary.
8. Command all pain to go.

BALANCE, LOSS OF (Also see Dizziness, Vertigo, and Meniere's Disease.)

Loss of Balance may be described as lightheadedness, being unsteady, feeling faint, dizziness, or vertigo (the room seems to be spinning or moving). Lightheadedness or Loss of Balance can occur when there is not enough blood getting to the brain. This can be caused by a sudden drop in blood pressure or dehydration following episodes of vomiting, diarrhea, fever, or other causes. Older people can experience this feeling if they change positions too quickly such as standing up from a lying or seated position (called Orthostatic Hypotension or Postural Hypotension). Lightheadedness often accompanies the flu, colds, allergies, motion sickness, or inner ear problems. It can also be a side effect of some medications, such as blood pressure pills or head injury.

How to Minister: (All commands done in Jesus' name.)
1. Rebuke the cause of the imbalance (for example, infection, disease, loss of sleep, etc.).
2. Command the neck to come into alignment.
3. Grow out the arms.
4. Command the balance center in the inner ear to be healed and the temporal bones to rotate back into position.

BALDNESS (Also called Alopecia.)

Partial or complete loss of hair is called Alopecia. Hair loss usually occurs gradually as a person ages. Normally, an individual

94

hair survives for an average of 4 1/2 years, grows about half an inch a month, falls out and is replaced by a new one within six months. Genetic Baldness is caused by the body's failure to produce new hairs and not by excessive hair loss. Hair loss can be caused by damage to the hair follicle from injury, medications, or disease such as chemotherapy for cancer.

How to Minister: (All commands done in Jesus' name.)

1. Command healing to the hair follicles and the blood to flow normally.
2. Command the hair be restored to normal amount.
3. Lead them in a prayer of repentance for generational curses.

BARRENNESS (See Infertility.)

BED-WETTING

Involuntary passage of urine at night by children over five to six years of age is called Bed-wetting. Children develop total control of their urinary bladders at different ages and nighttime dryness is usually the last stage of toilet training. When children wet the bed more than twice per month after age five or six, we call it Bed-wetting.

Children who were dry for at least six months and then started wetting again usually have secondary underlying problems. The problem might be physical or emotional, or just a change in sleep patterns. When the child is never dry overnight, their body is producing more urine than the bladder can hold while the child is in a deep sleep. The child's brain does not respond to the signal that the bladder is full during sleep. It is not the child's or the parent's fault. A child with this problem will very likely have a short leg.

How to Minister: (All commands done in Jesus' name.)

1. Grow out the legs.
2. Command the pelvis to come into alignment.
3. Command the vertebrae in the lower back to be adjusted, the nerves to the bladder to be released, the bladder to be healed and function properly.
4. Command the brain to awaken the child when the bladder is full.

BELL'S PALSY

Bell's Palsy is caused by damage to a cranial nerve and is characterized by a sudden facial drooping and a decreased ability to move some facial muscles. The cause is often not clear. It is thought that the disorder may be associated with inflammation of the facial nerve where it passes through the bones of the skull. Other conditions, such as Sarcoidosis, Diabetes, and Lyme disease, have been associated with Bell's Palsy and increased stress seems to aggravate the symptoms.

How to Minister: (All commands done in Jesus' name.)

1. Cast out the spirit of Bell's Palsy.
2. Command the pain to go.
3. Lay hands gently on the face, commanding the nerves to be regenerated and restored to perfect function.

BIPOLAR DISORDER (ALSO KNOWN AS MANIC-DEPRESSIVE.)

Bipolar Disorder (BD) is a malfunction of the brain that causes unpredictable mood swings. People with BD go from an emotional high (known as Mania) to a low (known as Depression). The disease randomly cycles between these highs and lows.

Women and men equally develop the condition usually between the ages of twenty and forty. Women spend more time in the depressed phase, while men may be manic (hyperactive) more often. Some people with BD have symptoms their entire lives, symptoms that can interfere with work and make relationships very difficult. In mania, people may not realize how dangerous their impulsive behaviors may be to themselves or to others.

How to Minister: (All commands done in Jesus' name.)

1. Lead them in a prayer of repentance for generational curses.
2. Lead them in a prayer of forgiveness from traumas suffered at a younger age.
3. Cast out the spirit of Bipolar Disorder.
4. Command the electrical and magnetic frequencies to be in harmony and balance.

BIRTH

How to Minister: (All commands done in Jesus' name.)

1. Pray for an easy delivery and a normal child.
2. Speak a blessing over a healthy, normal baby in the womb with the power of the Holy Spirit.
3. Lead parents in prayer to dedicate the child to God.
4. Command the pelvis to rotate in the perfect position for delivery.

BLADDER PROBLEMS (See Incontinence.)

BLADDER INFECTIONS (See Urinary Tract Infections.)

BLINDNESS

Blindness is a vision loss that is not correctable with glasses. Blindness can be partial (some objects or shapes can be distinguished) or complete (no perception of light). People with vision worse than 20/200 are considered legally blind.

Blindness has many causes. In the United States, the leading causes include diabetes, glaucoma, macular degeneration, and accidental injuries (chemical burns, bungee cords, fishing hooks, fireworks, racket balls, and similar objects). World statistics indicate the leading causes of blindness include cataracts, "river blindness," trachoma (a contagious bacterial disease of the eye), leprosy, and vitamin A deficiency.

How to Minister: (All commands done in Jesus' name.)

1. If the cause is known, address it specifically (such as glaucoma, cataracts, infection, detached retina, etc.).
2. Cast out the spirit of Blindness.
3. Command healing to the eyes and perfect sight to be restored.
4. Command a creative miracle to the nerves, eye structures, and brain.

BLOOD PRESSURE PROBLEMS

Blood Pressure is a measurement of the force applied to the walls of the arteries as the heart pumps blood through the body. Blood pressure is determined by the force and amount of blood pumped by the heart as well as the condition of the arteries (blood vessels carrying blood to the body). This pressure is affected by both the force and amount of blood pumped from the heart, and the size and flexibility of the arteries.

Blood pressure is continually changing depending on environment, activity, posture, dietary intake, temperature, emotions, physical health, disease processes, and medication use. Many other factors can affect blood pressure, including volume of liquid in the body, amount of sodium or salt in the body, kidney function, condition of the nervous system and blood vessels, arteriosclerosis, and various hormones in the body.

Problems develop from and/or can cause malfunction of other body organs when the blood pressure levels cannot return to or maintain normal levels. Ask if the doctor has diagnosed any possible underlying causes (such as diabetes, heart disease, arteriosclerosis, kidney problems, etc.).

Hypertension generally means the systolic pressure (upper number) is consistently over 140 and diastolic (lower number) blood pressure is consistently over 90. Hypertension can lead to stroke, heart attack, kidney damage, congestive heart disease, visual disturbances, severe headaches, and chest pain (angina).

Hypotension indicates blood pressure is lower than normal. This can lead to extreme weakness, organ damage and/or shutdown, unconsciousness and death. Abnormally low blood pressure can be caused by dehydration, anemia, hemorrhage, or medication side effects.

Orthostatic Hypotension or Postural Hypotension causes dizziness, lightheadedness, a feeling of fainting, and extreme weakness when a person changes positions (a change in posture such as moving from lying down to a sitting position or from sitting to standing). A fall with serious injury can result. This type of Hypotension is often a medication side effect. Changing positions slowly can minimize the effects of Postural Hypotension.

How to Minister: (All commands done in Jesus' name.)

1. Lead them in a prayer of repentance for generational curses.
2. Grow out the arms.
3. Command the entire vascular system to be healed, vessels be opened and function normally with proper elasticity and adequate blood flow.

4. Command the blood pressure to return to normal and to remain normal.
5. Command all organs and tissues damaged by the abnormal blood pressure to be healed and function normally.
6. Lead them in prayer to lay all their stress, cares, and worries on the altar of God.

BOWLEGGED

Knees and hips swing outward. A person with this problem has a "cowboy" look.

How to Minister: (All commands done in Jesus' name.)

1. Command the pelvis to come into normal alignment.
2. Grow out the legs.
3. Command the legs to straighten.

BPH (BENIGN PROSTATE HYPERTROPHY) (See Prostate Problems.)

BRAIN DAMAGE

The brain can be damaged at birth, from illness, injury, accident, disease (such as a stroke or a tumor), or lack of oxygen (from drowning or suffocation). Injuries to the brain and the nerves it controls causes loss of function such as decreased mentation (retardation, confusion, and memory loss), inability to control bodily functions or movement of arms and/or legs, paralysis, loss of speech, or inability to swallow safely.

How to Minister: (All commands done in Jesus' name.)

1. Lay hands on the head commanding a creative miracle—"a new brain."
2. Command all the nerves to function normally and any memory loss to be restored.
3. If caused by a stroke, command the spirit of death to go.

BREAST CANCER (ALSO SEE CANCER.)

An abnormal mass in the breast is usually diagnosed as a lump (or tumor). This can be a benign (harmless) tumor, which can be removed easily. A malignant tumor, however, can spread to other parts of the body destroying surrounding tissues, organs, and body functions. This abnormal growth of tissue found in a breast is called Breast Cancer, the second most common cancer affecting women in the United States. Although more common in women, Breast Cancer also can develop in men.

How to Minister: (All commands done in Jesus' name.)

1. Curse and cast out the spirit of Cancer.
2. Lead them in prayer of repentance for generational curses.
3. Lead them in prayer of repentance for bitterness or unforgiveness, if necessary.
4. Command electrical and magnetic frequencies to come into harmony and balance.
5. Curse any prions and command them to dissolve and be discarded by the body.
6. Command all damaged tissue be restored to normal healthy function.

BROKEN BONES

A break of any size is called a fracture. If the broken bone punctures the skin, it becomes a compound fracture. A stress fracture can occur in people with osteoporosis when a weakened area of bone simply breaks during normal movement or activities of the day or from a slight bump.

How to Minister: (All commands done in Jesus' name.)

1. Command the affected bones to come together in normal alignment and strength and be healed.

2. Command all muscles, tendons, nerves, and ligaments to line up with the healed bones and strength restored.
3. Rebuke trauma and command the pain to go.

BRONCHITIS

Bronchitis is an inflammation or infection of the main airways to the lungs (bronchus). Bronchitis may occur suddenly and last for a short time, or become chronic. To be classified as chronic, Bronchitis must cause a cough with mucus production most days of the month for three months out of the year. The disease process can change the body's normal functioning and often recurs.

How to Minister: (All commands done in Jesus' name.)

1. Rebuke the infection.
2. Lay hands on the upper chest and throat, commanding the tissues in the bronchial tubes and lungs to be healed and function normally.
3. Lead them in the prayer of repentance for any ungodly words spoken, if necessary.

BULIMIA

Bulimia is characterized by food binges or uncontrollable recurrent episodes of overeating. The person then uses vomiting or laxative abuse to prevent the food from staying in the body where it can be absorbed, be stored as fat, and increase body weight.

Many people with bulimia may also suffer from Anorexia Nervosa, an eating disorder involving severe weight loss that can lead to starvation.

How to Minister: (All commands done in Jesus' name.)

1. Lead them in prayer of repentance for their rebellion at adolescence.

2. Have them renounce the words spoken in rebellion.
3. Speak healing to areas of the body damaged by the abnormal eating behaviors.

BUNIONS

Bunions are often caused by narrow-toed, high-heeled, or ill-fitting shoes. The pressure against the big toe pushes it toward the second toe. This causes a marked protrusion at the base of the big toe. The condition may become painful as extra bone grows at the base of the big toe with a fluid build up over the area. This leads to swelling, increased pressure, and pain. Found more frequently in women, Bunions sometimes run in families.

How to Minister: (All commands done in Jesus' name.)

1. Lead them in a prayer of repentance for generational curses.
2. Rebuke the inflammation.
3. Grow out the legs.
4. Command the toe and bones to go back into place, the ligaments to strengthen and for the foot to be normal.

BURSITIS

Bursitis is an acute or chronic inflammation of the fluid-filled cushions that lie between tendons and bones. These fluid-filled sacs (called bursa) assist movement and reduce friction between moving parts. Bursitis can develop from chronic overuse, trauma, rheumatoid arthritis, or infection. Bursitis most commonly occurs in the shoulder, knee, elbow, and hip. The Achilles tendon and the foot may also be affected.

How to Minister: (All commands done in Jesus' name.)

1. Cast out the spirit of Bursitis.
2. Lead them in a prayer of forgiveness, if necessary.

3. Lay hands on the area and command all inflammation and pain to go.
4. Command the tissues to be healed, and normal fluid be produced for painless movements of the joints.

CANCER (Also see Breast Cancer, Tumor, Colorectal Cancer, and Leukemia.)

Cancer is the uncontrolled growth of abnormal cells that have mutated from normal tissues within the body. These abnormal cells can kill when the normal function of vital organs is interrupted. They can spread throughout the body, damaging and destroying essential systems. Cancer develops from normal cells from almost any organ or tissue of the body including the lung, colon, breast, skin, bones, or nerves. There are numerous types of diseases categorized as Cancer, which affect people of all ages.

How to Minister: (All commands done in Jesus' name.)

1. Curse the root of the cancer cells and cast out the spirit of cancer.
2. Lead them in a prayer of repentance for generational curses.
3. Lead them in prayer of repentance for bitterness or unforgiveness, if necessary.
4. Command electrical and magnetic frequencies to come into harmony and balance.
5. Curse any prions and command them to dissolve and be absorbed by the body.
6. Command the body's defensive "killer" cells to multiply, attack, and destroy all cancer cells.
7. Command healing to any damaged tissues and organs and normal function be restored.

CANDIDA ALBICANS (ALSO CALLED YEAST INFECTION.)

Yeast is an important and necessary part of the digestive process within the body. However, under certain circumstances, it can overgrow and cause problems. It is then considered a form of infection. A fungal (yeast) infection that affects the mucus membranes of the body is generally the cause of vaginal infections. It is aggravated by sugar intake and is the cause of thrush (a form of Candida) in newborns. It is also aggravated or exacerbated by antibiotics, birth control pills, and/or steroid usage. It can occur on external areas of the body that are dark, warm, and moist. Usually found in women, Candida can also affect men.

How to Minister: (All commands done in Jesus' name.)

1.   Rebuke the infection.
2.   Command the body's systems to be restored to normal function and yeast levels to be normal.
3.   Lead them in a prayer of repentance to break word curses.

CANKER SORES

Canker sores are ulcers found in the mouth and around the lips. They are NOT contagious. The cause may be related to a virus, a weakened immune system (for example, from a cold or the flu), hormonal changes, mechanical irritation, stress, or low levels of vitamin B-12.

Women seem to get Canker Sores more often than men. Mouth sores can be a sign of an underlying illness, tumor, allergic reaction, or effects from a medication.

How to Minister: (All commands done in Jesus' name.)

1.   Rebuke any infection or virus and curse the root.
2.   Command the immune system to be strengthened and to function properly.

105

3. Command the electrical and magnetic frequencies to be in harmony and balance.
4. Command all pain and discomfort to disappear.
5. Command all affected tissues to be healed and function normally.

CARPAL TUNNEL SYNDROME

Carpal Tunnel Syndrome is a compression of a nerve at the wrist, which may result in numbness, tingling, weakness, or muscle atrophy (shrinking) in the hand and fingers. When the wrist is poorly positioned, the nerve that passes through the "Carpal Tunnel" passageway from the arm to the hand is pinched. Any swelling or irritation in this area can cause compression of the nerve. This interruption of the nerve function hinders the sensation and movement of the hand.

The condition occurs most often in people over thirty and is more common in women than men. This syndrome is common in people who perform repetitive motions of the hand and wrist, such as typing. Associated conditions include pregnancy, premenstrual syndrome (PMS), and menopause probably because hormonal changes can cause fluid retention and swelling of the tissues.

How to Minister: (All commands done in Jesus' name.)

1. Lay hands on the wrist area and command the tissues, tendons, and ligaments in the wrist to be healed and relaxed.
2. Command the "tunnel" to open up and pressure on the nerves to be released.
3. Command normal circulation and strength to be restored.
4. Command any numbness and tingling to leave and the wrist to be healed and to function normally.

CATARACTS

The lens of an eye is normally clear. If the lens becomes cloudy, the condition is known as a Cataract. Cataracts can progress or "grow" until total blindness occurs. They are removed surgically.

Adult Cataracts usually develop with advancing age, may run in families, and are accelerated by environmental factors such as smoking or exposure to other toxic substances. They may develop after an eye injury. Metabolic diseases such as diabetes increase the risk for Cataracts. Congenital Cataracts may be inherited and are present at or shortly after birth.

How to Minister: (All commands done in Jesus' name.)

1. Lay hands on eyes and command the cataracts to dissolve.
2. Command the blood and fluid to flow through the eye layers normally.
3. Lead them in a prayer of repentance for generational curses.

CEREBRAL PALSY (Also called CP or Spastic Paralysis.)

Cerebral Palsy is a group of neurological disorders characterized by loss of control of movements or nerve functions. These disorders are caused by injuries to the portion of the brain that is involved with higher mental faculties, sensations, and voluntary muscle activities. The injury occurs during fetal development or near the time of birth.

Initially, Cerebral Palsy was thought to be related to lack of oxygen to the brain at birth, but it has now been shown that this is an uncommon cause of Cerebral Palsy. Affected brain areas receive lower levels of oxygen at some point, but the exact cause has not been identified. A form of Cerebral Palsy can also occur with brain damage after an illness or injury.

107

How to Minister: (All commands done in Jesus' name.)

1. Cast out the spirit of Cerebral Palsy.
2. Speak a new brain into the body.
3. Command normal communication from the brain to the other body parts.
4. Command the muscles, tendons, and nerves to function properly.
5. Lead them in a prayer of repentance for generational curses.

CHOLESTEROL, HIGH (Also called Hyperlipidemia.)

Cholesterol is a substance found in all parts of the body tissues of both humans and animals. Called a lipid (blood fat), it is manufactured in the liver for normal body functions including the production of hormones, bile, and Vitamin D. The blood transports cholesterol to all parts of the body.

Sufficient cholesterol is actually made by the liver for the body's needs. Cholesterol is found in foods from animal sources such as eggs, meat, poultry, and dairy products. Excessive intake of saturated fats (that turn to cholesterol) can damage one's health. High Cholesterol levels can contribute to the development of Arteriosclerosis, which can lead to disorders such as stroke and heart attack. (Also see Arteriosclerosis.)

How to Minister: (All commands done in Jesus' name.)

1. Lead them in pray of repentance for improper diet, if necessary.
2. Command the cholesterol level to return to normal and the body to retain only the necessary amount.
3. Lay hands on the person's head, commanding all potentially damaged parts of the body (arteries, heart, etc.) to be healed and to function normally.

CHRONIC OBSTRUCTIVE PULMONARY DISEASE

Chronic Obstructive Pulmonary Disease (COPD) is a group of lung diseases characterized by abnormal airflow and varying degrees of air sac changes, airway inflammation, and lung tissue destruction.

The leading cause of COPD is smoking, which often leads to the two most common forms of this disease: Emphysema (enlarged air sacs of the lung, and reduced lung tissue elasticity) and Chronic Bronchitis (lung inflammation, air sac destruction, and narrowed airways).

Other risk factors for COPD are secondhand smoke and working in a polluted environment. Occupational Lung Disease (Asbestosis, Silicosis, and Coal Miner's disease) are other forms of COPD. The degree of airway obstruction and the amount of tissue damage in the lung passages determine the severity of the illness.

How to Minister: (All commands done in Jesus' name.)

1. Curse the root of the disease.
2. Lead them in a prayer of repentance, if necessary. (For smoking, see Addictions)
3. Command total healing to all damaged tissues of the respiratory system and normal function be restored.
4. Command new lungs, if necessary.

CIGARETTES (SEE ADDICTIONS.)

CLEFT LIP/CLEFT PALATE

Cleft Lip and/or Cleft Palate are abnormalities of the upper lip, and the hard and soft palate of the mouth and are present from before birth. These developmental abnormalities may range from a small notch in the upper lip to a complete opening extending into the roof of the mouth and nose. These malformations may occur separately or together.

Cleft Lip and Cleft Palate may be seen in association with other birth defects or syndromes. There are numerous causes for these birth defects, including mutant genes, drugs, viruses, or other toxins that can cause abnormal fetal development. As well as being disfiguring, these abnormalities can cause feeding difficulties, speech development problems, and recurrent ear infections.

How to Minister: (All commands done in Jesus' name.)

1. Lead then in a prayer of repentance for generational curses.
2. Lay hands on the mouth, commanding a creative miracle with all the tissues and affected structures to be normal.
3. Command any pain to go.

COLD SORES (See Herpes.)

COLDS (See also Sore Throat, Influenza, Croup, and Laryngitis.)

A common Cold is an infection of the upper respiratory tract. It includes symptoms of runny nose, sore throat, cough, watery eyes, sneezing, congestion, and a fever less than 102 degrees F. Any one of more than 200 viruses can cause a common cold. Most adults will have a common cold two to four times a year while children may have a common cold as many as eight to ten times a year.

In adults or children, a common Cold that does not resolve readily may lead to Sinusitis, Croup, Otitis Media (ear infection), or Laryngitis. Other secondary infections that may develop following a common Cold include Strep Throat, Chronic

Bronchitis, and/or Pneumonia. A Cold may also be referred to as an Upper Respiratory Infection.

Adults may simply have a Cold with Laryngitis, but children can develop Croup.

Croup is an inflammation of the voice box (larynx) and the airway just beneath it. A child may have a common cold for several days and then unexpectedly develop a loud, barking cough. The swelling and narrowing of the air passages makes breathing difficult. Croup primarily affects younger and smaller children because their small airways are more susceptible to narrowing when inflamed.

How to Minister: (All commands done in Jesus' name.)

1. Rebuke the infection and curse the root of it.
2. Command the immune system to be strengthened and to function properly.
3. Command the electrical and magnetic frequencies to be in harmony and balance.
4. Command all pain and discomfort to disappear.
5. Command all affected tissues to be healed and function normally.

COLITIS

Colitis is an inflammation of the large intestine that can be caused by many different disease processes including acute and chronic infections, inflammatory disorders (such as ulcerative colitis or Crohn's disease), interruption or lack of blood flow, and/or a history of radiation to the large bowel.

How to Minister: (All commands done in Jesus' name.)

1. Grow out the legs (do the leg adjustment).
2. Command the nerves, tissues, and muscles of the colon to function normally.

3. Command all inflammation to leave and the colon to be healed.
4. Lead them in a prayer to lay all cares, stress, and worries on the altar of God.

COLORECTAL CANCER (Also see Cancer, Tumor.)

The colon and rectum are part of the large intestine (large bowel). Colon and rectal cancers, sometimes referred to as "Colorectal Cancer," develop from the lining of the large intestine. When cancer starts on the surface lining of an organ like the large intestine, it is called a carcinoma.

Other types of colon cancer include lymphoma, carcinoid tumors, melanoma, and sarcomas. Even though Colorectal Cancer is the second leading cause of cancer deaths, this disease is entirely treatable if caught early by regular examinations. There is no single cause for colon cancer. However, many colon cancers begin as benign polyps and then eventually develop into cancer.

How to Minister: (All commands done in Jesus' name.)

1. Curse the root of the cancer cells and cast out the spirit of cancer.
2. Lead them in a prayer of repentance for generational curses.
3. Lead them in a prayer for repentance for bitterness or unforgiveness, if necessary.
4. Command electrical and magnetic frequencies to come into harmony and balance.
5. Curse any prions and command them to dissolve and be discarded by the body.
6. Command the body's defensive "killer" cells to multiply, attack, and destroy all cancer cells.
7. Command all damaged tissues to be healed and to function normally.

COMA

A Coma is a state of deep unconsciousness. Causes can include intoxication (drug, alcohol, or toxin), metabolic abnormalities, seizure activity such as epilepsy, head injury, shock, lack of oxygen, and low blood pressure. Unusual and unexpected episodes of decreased consciousness, unconsciousness, and Coma require prompt medical attention and professional evaluation.

How to Minister: (All commands done in Jesus' name.)

1. Cast out the spirit of death of brain cells.
2. Lay hands on the head, commanding the brain to be healed.
3. Command a creative miracle to any damaged brain tissue (brain tissue will not regenerate on its own).
4. Command the body and all its organs to function normally and consciousness to return.

CONGESTIVE HEART FAILURE (CHF) (SEE HEART.)

CONSTIPATION

Constipation refers to the passing of infrequent or difficult bowel movements. Constipation may cause pain during the passage of a bowel movement, includes the inability to pass a bowel movement after straining or pushing for more than ten minutes, or no bowel movements for several days. Infants may go seven days without a stool if they are exclusively breastfed; however, this is uncommon.

Constipation is most often caused by a low-fiber diet, lack of physical activity, and/or not drinking enough water. Stress and travel can also contribute to constipation or changes in bowel habits. Diseases of the bowel (such as irritable bowel syndrome or

Crohn's disease), pregnancy, certain medical conditions, mental health problems, neurological diseases, high stress, or medications may contribute to constipation.

How to Minister: (All commands done in Jesus' name.)

1. Command the colon to function normally.
2. Lead them in a prayer of repentance, if necessary.
3. Lead them in a prayer of repentance for improper diet, if necessary.
4. Lead them in prayer to lay all cares, stress, fears and worries on the altar of God.

CORNS AND CALLUSES

Corns and Calluses are thickened layers of skin caused by repeated pressure or friction. A Corn is thickened skin on the top or side of a toe, usually from shoes that do not fit properly. Corns can be very painful when touched.

A Callus is thickened skin on your hands or the soles of your feet. The thickening of the skin is a protective reaction to prevent skin breakdown from repeated friction to the area. Both Calluses and Corns can be removed by a qualified Podiatrist, but can recur.

How to Minister: (All commands done in Jesus' name.)

1. Lay hands on the affected area, commanding the Corns and Calluses to fall off and not return.
2. Command the Callus be replaced by healthy tissue.

CROHN'S DISEASE

Crohn's Disease is a chronic autoimmune disease that can affect any part of the gastrointestinal tract but most commonly occurs in the area where the small and large intestine meet. In

Crohn's Disease, rogue immune cells attack the gastrointestinal system. The cause is unknown.

Inflammation may affect any area of the digestive tract. As a result of the immune attack, the intestinal wall becomes thick, and deep ulcers may form. This can lead to severe pain and obstruction.

The disease may occur at any age, but adolescents and young adults are at the highest risk. Because of the debilitating effects of this disease, some people elect to have a portion of the bowel removed and live with a colostomy the rest of their lives.

How to Minister: (All commands done in Jesus' name.)

1. Cast out the spirit of Crohn's disease.
2. Rebuke the infection.
3. Command the bowel tissue to be healed and function normally.
4. Lead them in a prayer of repentance for generational curses.
5. Command the immune system to function normally.

CROSS-EYED OR WALLEYED (ALSO CALLED STRABISMUS.)

A deviation of the alignment of one eye in relation to the other is called Strabismus. Because of the lack of coordination between the eyes or uneven development of the muscles that control eye movements, the eyes look in different directions and do not focus at the same time on a single object. The cause is unknown and is usually present at or shortly after birth.

When the two eyes fail to focus on the same object, the brain can ignore the input from one eye. If this is allowed to continue, the eye that the brain ignores will never function normally. When the eyes look outward, it is called Walleyed. When they look inward, it is called Cross-eyed.

How to Minister: (All commands done in Jesus' name.)

1. Place your hands over the eyes and command the muscles, ligaments, and tissues to be healed and return to normal strength and length.
2. Lead them in a prayer of repentance for generational curses.
3. Command the brain to function normally and process the input from both eyes.
4. Command any scar tissue to be removed.

CROUP (See Cold.)

CUSHING'S SYNDROME

Cushing's Syndrome is a metabolic disorder that is caused by elevated levels of an important hormone over an extended period of time. Adrenal tumors, which may be benign or malignant, can be a cause of the elevated levels of this hormone.

Other causes of Cushing's Syndrome can include a pituitary tumor, another malfunctioning organ of the body, or regular use of steroids such as prednisone which is commonly used to treat chronic conditions such as rheumatoid arthritis and COPD.

How to Minister: (All commands done in Jesus' name.)

1. Cast out the spirit of Cushing's Syndrome.
2. Lay hands on the kidney area of the back (approximately at waist level) commanding the adrenal glands to function normally.
3. Lead them in a prayer of repentance, if necessary.

CVA or Cardiovascular Accident (See Stroke.)

CYSTIC DISEASE

This condition affects women, usually near or at menopause; and is characterized by a rapid development of cysts in the breasts. It is also called fibrocystic disease or cystic mastitis.

How to Minister: (All commands done in Jesus' name.)

1. Cast out the spirit of fibrocystic disease.
2. Lay hands on chest, commanding all the cysts to dissolve. (Have the person lay their hands on their chest first, then lay your hands on top of theirs.)
3. Command all the cells and tissues of the breast to be healed and normal, and a creative miracle for any damaged parts.

CYSTIC FIBROSIS

Cystic Fibrosis is an inherited disease that causes breathing and digestive problems. It affects the mucus and sweat glands as well. Thick mucus formed in the breathing passages of the lungs increases the risk for chronic lung infections. Many pancreatic enzymes involved in the metabolism and usage of fat in the intestines are absent. Inadequate absorption of nutrients from the intestinal tract leads to malnutrition.

How to Minister: (All commands done in Jesus' name.)

1. Lead them in a prayer of repentance for generational curses.
2. Cast out the spirit of Cystic Fibrosis.
3. Lay hands on the area of the pancreas and liver, commanding the glands of the body to secrete enzymes normally and metabolism to return to normal.
4. Command the lungs, pancreas, and liver to be healed and function normally.

DEAF-MUTE

A person who can neither hear nor speak is said to be a Deaf-Mute. Since these conditions limit learning capacity, these people may seem to be mentally challenged, as well. Helen Keller was both deaf and mute, but is well known for her remarkable accomplishments after her specialized education.

How to Minister: (All commands done in Jesus' name.)

1. Cast out the deaf and dumb spirit.
2. Continue with the instructions for Deafness.
3. Lead them in a prayer of repentance for generational curses.

DEAFNESS

Deafness (hearing loss) is the inability to hear sound adequately in one or both ears. A small decrease in hearing is normal after age twenty. There are many causes of hearing loss. Conductive loss occurs because of a mechanical problem, such as fluid in the ear or a broken eardrum. Nerve loss occurs when the nerve from the ear to the brain is damaged and cannot communicate impulses or sounds. Conductive loss is often medically reversible—nerve loss is not.

Ear infections are the most common cause of temporary hearing loss in children. Fluid can linger in the ear following an ear infection. Although this fluid can go unnoticed, it can cause significant hearing problems in children. Excessive wax buildup in the ear canal can block sound and simulate a hearing loss. Listening to very loud music over a period of time can damage these structures and nerves also.

How to Minister: (All commands done in Jesus' name.)

1. Cast out the spirit of Deafness.
2. Put your fingers gently in the person's ears and command the deafness to go and hearing to be restored.
3. Grow out their arms (do the arm adjustment).
4. Command a new eardrum and bone structures, if needed.

5. Command the nerves and muscles to relax, releasing the nerves to the ears and allowing the blood to flow normally into the area. Command the hair-like nerves to the inner ear to function normally.

6. Place the hands on the sides of the skull and command the temporal bones to rotate back into position.

7. Test the person's hearing and repeat the above steps, if necessary.

DEEP VEIN THROMBOSIS (ALSO CALLED DVT.)

Deep Venous Thrombosis describes a blood clot (thrombus) that has developed in a large vein located deep within a leg or thigh. The blood clot interferes with the circulation of the area causing swelling, pain, and damage to the surrounding tissues. It can travel through the blood stream until it lodges in the brain, lungs, heart, or other areas, causing severe complications such as a stroke or heart attack.

Thrombophlebitis is another term used in this category although it can occur in small veins also. Thrombophlebitis means an irritation or inflammation within the blood vessel caused by a thrombus (blood clot).

Risks include prolonged sitting, bed rest or immobilization such as long plane or car trips, recent surgery, childbirth within the last six months, and the use of medications such as birth control pills.

How to Minister: (All commands done in Jesus' name.)

1. Command the blood clot to dissolve.
2. Command the blood to flow properly and all damaged tissues to be healed and function normally.
3. Lead them in a prayer of repentance for generational curses.

DEGENERATIVE JOINT DISEASE (SEE OSTEOARTHRITIS.)

DEPRESSION (SEE ALSO POSTPARTUM DEPRESSION.)

Depression may be described as feeling sad, blue, unhappy, miserable, or "down in the dumps." Most of us feel this way at one time or another for short periods. Clinical Depression is a mood disorder in which feelings of sadness, loss, anger, or frustration interfere with everyday life over an extended period of time.

Depression can be mild, moderate, or severe and last from a few hours or days to years. Some symptoms can include insomnia, excessive sleeping, a dramatic change in appetite, fatigue, lack of energy, agitation, restlessness, irritability, inactivity, withdrawal from usual activities, feelings of hopelessness, and recurring thoughts of death or suicide

Low self-esteem is common with Depression. So are sudden bursts of anger and lack of pleasure from activities that normally cause joy or happiness. It is usually a stressful, unhappy, traumatic life event that triggers the onset of a depressive episode.

How to Minister: (All commands done in Jesus' name.)

1. Take your time and love them with the love of the Lord.
2. If possible, identify the cause and when it started.
3. Lead them in a prayer of repentance or forgiveness, if necessary.
4. Command the electrical and magnetic frequencies to be in harmony and balance.
5. With your hand on their heart, command the spirit of Depression to go.
6. Speak peace and joy to them.

DERMATITIS (ALSO SEE ECZEMA.)

Dermatitis is an inflammation of the skin.

How to Minister: (All commands done in Jesus' name.)

1. Rebuke the infection or irritation.
2. Command the itching to stop.
3. Command cells that manufacture skin to create new and healthy tissue.

DETACHED RETINA

Retinal Detachment is a separation of the light-sensitive tissue membrane in the back of the eye from the eye's underlying layers. This transparent membrane at the back of the eye processes visual images focused on it by the cornea and the lens and communicates what is seen to the brain. Retinal Detachment can be caused by trauma, the aging, diabetes, or an inflammation, but it can occur spontaneously. Initially, it severely limits central vision leaving peripheral vision only; however it can lead to irreversible blindness.

How to Minister: (All commands done in Jesus' name.)

1. Lay hands on the eye(s) and command the retina and its nerve endings to reconnect to the eye and be healed.
2. Command the eye to function normally and eyesight to be restored to normal.

DIABETES MELLITUS

Diabetes is a disease marked by high levels of sugar (or glucose) in the bloodstream. It can be caused by too little insulin produced by the pancreas to regulate blood sugar, resistance to insulin, or both.

Glucose is a form of sugar ingested with food and fluids. It is absorbed during digestion and is delivered by the blood to all the cells of the body. The pancreas produces insulin to regulate the amount of glucose in the bloodstream. All body cells require a certain level of glucose to maintain their normal function.

People with Diabetes have high, uncontrolled blood glucose levels. Left uncontrolled, Diabetes can contribute to blindness, kidney disease, neuropathy (numbness and pain in all extremities), and circulation problems. If the levels are too high or too low, death can result.

How to Minister: (All commands done in Jesus' name.)

1. Cast out the spirit of diabetes.
2. Lead them in a prayer of repentance for generational curses.
3. Command a new pancreas into the body that will produce enough insulin to control and use blood sugar normally.
4. Command any damaged body parts (from excess sugar) to be healed and made whole.

DIARRHEA

Diarrhea is the frequent passing of loose, watery bowel movements. Diarrhea is considered chronic when loose or frequent stools have occurred for longer than four weeks.

The most common cause is a mild viral infection that can resolve spontaneously within a few days. This is often called "stomach flu" and can appear in mini-epidemics in schools, neighborhoods or families. It is often passed from person to person. Hand washing after toileting can diminish the risk.

Uncontrolled diarrhea can lead to severe dehydration, metabolic imbalances, and rectal bleeding. Uncontrolled diarrhea in small children can be fatal.

How to Minister: (All commands done in Jesus' name.)

1. Command the pelvis to come into alignment.

2. Command digestive system to be healed and to function normally.
3. Rebuke any possible infection.

DISC PROBLEMS (ALSO SEE BACK PROBLEMS.)

This is commonly called "slipped disc." The disc (or cushion) between two vertebrae (bones in the spine) has either deteriorated or is bulging out, pressing on a nerve and causing discomfort and pain.

How to Minister: (All commands done in Jesus' name.)

1. Minister as you would for Back Pain and command the disc to be restored, be healed, and recreated if necessary; command all pressure on the nerves to be released and all inflammation and swelling to go.
2. Command the vertebrae to be healed, rotated back into place, bones to come together if fractured, ribs to be healed and go back into place and all pain to leave.

DIVERTICULOSIS/DIVERTICULITIS

Small bulging areas of the inner lining of the intestine (called Diverticula) can develop in any part of the bowel. Diverticulosis indicates the presence of Diverticula. Diverticulitis is an inflammation of these sacs, bulges, or pouches of the intestinal wall. It can cause severe abdominal pain, fever, constipation, or perforation (a hole through the colon lining). If the perforation is large, stool in the colon can leak into the abdominal cavity causing a very serious, life-threatening condition.

How to Minister: (All commands done in Jesus' name.)

1. Command the pelvis to come into proper alignment.
2. Command the sacs to disappear and the bowel wall to return to normal strength and function.

123

3. Lead them in a prayer of repentance and place all their stress, worries, and cares on the altar of God.
4. Command infection to go and tissues to be totally healed.

DIZZINESS (Also see Vertigo.)

Dizziness is a common neurological symptom. The most common form of severe Dizziness is known as Vertigo. This term describes a sensation of motion when there is no motion or an exaggerated sense of motion in response to certain body movements.

Both symptoms are linked to inner ear disturbances as well as a variety of other illnesses. The sensation of Dizziness is frequently accompanied by other symptoms such as unsteadiness, anxiety, lightheadedness, and loss of balance. The causes range from infections to fatigue to allergies. A common description may be "My head is spinning." It can also be a symptom of a low heart rate, low blood pressure, or medication side effects.

How to Minister: (All commands done in Jesus' name.)

1. Command the electrical and magnetic frequencies to be in harmony and in balance.
2. Command the fluid in the inner ear to return to normal.
3. Command normal balance to return and any underlying causes to disappear.

DJD (Degenerative Joint Disease. See Osteoarthritis.)

DOWN SYNDROME

Down Syndrome is a chromosome abnormality, usually due to an extra copy of the 21st chromosome. This syndrome can result in abnormal body function development.

Children with Down Syndrome have a widely recognized and characteristic appearance. The head may be smaller than

124

normal with abnormally shaped facial features including a flattened nose, protruding tongue, and upward slanting eyes. The hands are short and broad with short fingers and a single crease in the palm. Retardation of normal growth and development is typical and most affected children do not reach average adult height.

How to Minister: (All commands done in Jesus' name.)

1. Cast out the spirit of Down Syndrome.
2. Lay hands on the person's head and command a new brain.
3. Command the cells to revert to the correct number of chromosomes and for the extra chromosome to go.
4. Command the body to be healed and function normally.
5. Command the facial features to be normal.

DROWNING

Drowning is death by suffocation from being immersed in liquid. The lack of oxygen causes the lungs and heart to stop functioning. After a few minutes without oxygen, brain damage occurs and death can follow. Immediate resuscitation can minimize permanent damage and prevent death.

How to Minister: (All commands done in Jesus' name.)

1. Cast out the spirit of death.
2. Command the liquid to come out of the lungs.
3. Command life to the body.
4. Command the brain and body to function normally and be totally healed.

DRY EYES

Dry Eyes are caused by a lack of tears, the clear liquid necessary for the lubrication of the eye. Tears wash away foreign particles. People with Dry Eyes will feel a burning, scratching, or stinging sensation. Dry Eyes can lead to tiny abrasions on the surface of the eyes.

How to Minister: (All commands done in Jesus' name.)

1. Command any blockage or abnormality to be gone and healing to take place.
2. Command the glands to produce normal amounts of fluid to keep the eyes healthy.

DUCK FEET

Feet turned excessively outward.

How to Minister: (All commands done in Jesus' name.)

1. Lead them in a prayer of repentance for generational curses.
2. Command the pelvic bones to adjust to proper position.
3. Command the hips, legs, and feet to return to normal position and be totally healed.

DYSLEXIA

Developmental Reading Disorder, also called Dyslexia, is a reading disability. People with this problem cannot process graphic symbols. Also called DRD, it is not caused by vision problems, but rather is a problem involving higher brain functions. Children with DRD may have trouble rhyming, separating sounds in spoken words, and learning to read.

Most children found with DRD have normal if not above average intelligence. Children with DRD may also have developmental writing disorder and/or developmental arithmetic disorder. All of these areas of thinking involve the manipulation of symbols to convey information.

How to Minister: (All commands done in Jesus' name.)

1. Command the nerves of the eyes to function normally and to send proper messages to the brain.
2. Lead them in a prayer of repentance for generational curses.
3. Command the brain to interpret the signals received and allow complete understanding.

EAR INFECTION (See Otitis Media.)

ECZEMA (Also see Dermatitis.)

Eczema is a chronic skin disorder, a form of dermatitis. It manifests as scaly and itchy rashes. People with Eczema often have a family history of allergic conditions. The inflammation and chronic irritation and scratching causes the skin to thicken and become leathery. Environmental irritants, dryness of the skin, exposure to water, temperature changes, and stress can all exacerbate the symptoms.

How to Minister: (All commands done in Jesus' name.)

1. Cast out the spirit of Eczema.
2. Command the inflammation to go and curse the infirmity.
3. Lead them in a prayer of repentance for generational curses.
4. Command the cells that manufacture skin to replace the damaged tissues, and the skin to return to normal structure, function, and texture.
5. Command the itching to go.

EDEMA

Edema or swelling can occur anywhere in the body. Swelling is a normal body response to an injury but should disappear as healing occurs (such as a sprained ankle). Edema can be a symptom of a chronic and progressive medical illness such as Congestive Heart Failure. It is caused by excessive buildup of fluid in the tissues that causes a rapid increase in weight over a short period of time. This swelling can be generalized (all over the body) or localized (legs and feet).

Lymphedema is a persistent swelling, a form of edema resulting from the interruption or loss of normal lymph drainage of the affected arm or leg. It can occur as a result of a mastectomy (removal of a breast) when numerous lymph nodes are also removed. This interruption of the lymph drainage system causes a backup of lymph fluid into the arm, which, in turn, causes a severely enlarged arm and hand. It can occur in all limbs, is difficult to treat, and can be severely debilitating.

How to Minister: (All commands done in Jesus' name.)

1. Command healing for any underlying disease.
2. Command that the involved organs or tissues be healed and function normally.
3. Command the fluid to pass out through the body.
4. Lead them in a prayer of repentance, if necessary.
5. Lead them in a prayer of repentance for generational curses.

EMPHYSEMA (ALSO SEE COPD.)

Emphysema is a lung condition that involves damage to the air sacs of the lungs. The air sacs are unable to completely empty and are therefore unable to refill with fresh air to ensure adequate oxygen supply to the body. Tobacco smoke and other pollutants release chemicals that damage the walls of the air sacs within the lungs. This damage becomes worse over time affecting the exchange of oxygen and carbon dioxide in the lungs. Cigarette smoking is the most common cause of Emphysema.

How to Minister: (All commands done in Jesus' name.)

1. Lead them in a prayer of repentance from smoking, if necessary. (See Addiction.)

2. Command a creative miracle: "a new set of lungs."
3. Command other damaged body tissue to be healed and function normally.

ENCEPHALITIS

Encephalitis is an inflammation, irritation, and swelling of the brain usually caused by a viral infection. Exposure to the virus can occur through insect bites, contaminated food or drink, inhaling respiratory droplets from an infected person, or skin contact. The inflammation can cause neurological or mental deterioration, confusion, or coma. It can be fatal.

How to Minister: (All commands done in Jesus' name.)
1. Rebuke the infection.
2. Command the swelling to go and the brain to be healed, restored, and function normally.
3. Pray for the neck to come into proper alignment.
4. Command the blood to flow normally within the brain.

ENDOMETRIOSIS (See Female Problems.)

END-STAGE RENAL DISEASE (See Kidney Failure.)

ENLARGED PROSTATE (See Prostate Problems.)

EPILEPSY

Epilepsy is a brain disorder characterized by periodic loss or impairment of consciousness often accompanied by convulsions or seizures. These episodes of disturbed brain function are caused by abnormal electrical discharges through the nerves in the brain. They usually last short periods of time and occasionally are undetected.

Epileptic seizures can be related to drugs, abnormal levels of sodium or glucose, head injury, or inherited abnormality. Often, the condition can be triggered by flashing lights.

How to Minister: (All commands done in Jesus' name.)
1. Cast out the spirit of Epilepsy.
2. Command the electrical and magnetic frequencies to be in harmony and balance.
3. Lead them in a prayer of repentance when necessary.
4. Command new brain tissues to develop and work normally.

EPSTEIN-BARR (SEE MONONUCLEOSIS.)

ESSENTIAL TREMOR (SEE TREMOR.)

FARSIGHTEDNESS

Farsightedness describes a problem with vision. Nearby objects do not appear clearly. The image is not focused properly on the retina of the eye.

Children outgrow the condition; however, as aging occurs, glasses or contact lenses may be required to correct the problem.

How to Minister: (All commands done in Jesus' name.)
1. Lay hands on the eyes, commanding the lens, nerves, ligaments, and muscles to be adjusted and work properly.
2. Command the eyeballs to be restored to their perfect size and function normally.
3. Command perfect sight to be restored.
4. Lead them in a prayer of repentance for generational curses.

FEAR

This is an abnormal fright of normal situations, people, and/ or things.

How to Minister: (All commands done in Jesus' name.)

1. If possible, identify how and when it started.
2. Lead them in a prayer of repentance or forgiveness when necessary.
3. Cast out the spirit of fear.
4. Lead them in a prayer to lay all cares, worries, and fears on the altar of God.
5. Speak peace to them.

FEET (Also see Bunions, Corns and Calluses, Gout, Pigeon Toes, and Hammer Toes.)

Most foot problems are inherited or from an injury, however they can also be a birth defect such as club feet.

How to Minister: (All commands done in Jesus' name.)

1. Command the twenty-six bones in each foot to go into proper position and be healed and strong.
2. Lead them in a prayer of repentance for generational curses.
3. Command any infection to go.
4. Command all injury/scarring to be healed.

FEMALE PROBLEMS (Also see Endometriosis, Fibroid Tumors, PMS and Prolapsed Uterus.)

This includes any problem with the female reproductive organs of the body. It includes painful menstrual periods, PMS (Premenstrual Syndrome), endometriosis, amenorrhea (absence of periods for six months or longer), and prolapsed uterus.

How to Minister: (All commands done in Jesus' name.)

1. Command all the tissues, nerves, and vessels to function normally,
2. Command the pelvis to go into proper alignment. (Do the pelvis adjustment.)

3. Command the sacrum to rotate into correct position.
4. Command any infection or irritation to go.
5. Command any scar tissue and damaged or destroyed parts to be restored and function properly.
6. Command all hormones to be in balance.
7. Command the electrical and magnetic frequencies to be in harmony and balance.

ENDOMETRIOSIS

Endometriosis is a condition in which the endometrium, tissue that normally lines the uterus, grows in other areas of the body causing pain, irregular bleeding, and infertility. The tissue growth typically occurs in the pelvic area, outside of the uterus, on the ovaries, bowel, rectum, bladder, or the lining of the pelvis, but it can occur in other areas of the body as well.

The cause of endometriosis is unknown. The scarring and adhesions that result from this disease process can cause infertility.

How to Minister: (All commands done in Jesus' name.)

1. Lead them in a prayer of repentance for generational curses.
2. Command the female organs to function normally.
3. Command the pelvis to come into proper alignment.
4. Command the extra tissues and scarring to dissolve.

FIBROID TUMORS

Fibroids are benign (noncancerous) tumors of the uterus. Unpredictable in size and behavior, fibroids can be as tiny as a pencil point or as large as a grapefruit, growing slowly or rapidly, either alone or in groups. As the tumors grow, women experience symptoms such as heavy menstrual periods; breakthrough bleeding; pelvic or abdominal pain and pressure; backache;

constipation; bladder pressure; and urinary incontinence, frequency, or retention.

How to Minister: (All commands done in Jesus' name.)

1. Command the pain and cramping to cease.
2. Command the spirit causing the tumor(s) to go.
3. Command the tumor cells to die and dissolve.
4. Command the pelvis to come into proper alignment.
5. Command the tissues of the reproductive organs be restored to normal function and be totally healed.

MENOPAUSE

Menopause is the transition period of a woman's life when the ovaries stop producing eggs, her body produces less estrogen and progesterone, and menstruation becomes less frequent, eventually stopping altogether. A natural event that normally occurs between the ages of 45 and 55, once Menopause is complete (called postmenopausal), a woman can no longer become pregnant.

The symptoms of Menopause are caused by changes in estrogen and progesterone levels. A gradual decrease of estrogen generally allows the body to slowly adjust to these hormonal changes. When estrogen drops suddenly (as when the ovaries are removed surgically), symptoms can be more severe. Hot and cold flashes, sensitivity to heat or cold, and emotional or behavior changes are but a few of the unpleasant symptoms women go through during Menopause.

How to Minister: (All commands done in Jesus' name.)

1. Command all the symptoms (hot flashes, sweats, etc.) to go.
2. Command the hormones to be in balance.

3. Command the electrical and magnetic frequencies to be in harmony and balance.
4. Lead them in a prayer of repentance for generational curses.
5. Command the pelvis to come into alignment.

MENSTRUAL PAIN (DYSMENORRHEA.)

Menstruation can be accompanied by sharp, intermittent or dull, aching pain usually in the pelvis or lower abdomen. Painful Menstruation affects many women and can cause difficulty with normal household, job, or school-related activities during the menstrual cycle.

Although some discomfort during Menstruation can be normal, excessive pain is not. Dysmenorrhea refers to Menstrual Pain severe enough to limit normal activities or to require some form of medication. Menstrual Pain may be accompanied by nausea, vomiting, constipation, or diarrhea.

How to Minister: (All commands done in Jesus' name.)

1. Lead them in a prayer of repentance for generational curses.
2. Command the pelvis to go into alignment.
3. Command the hormones to be in balance.
4. Command all pain to leave.

PREMENSTRUAL SYNDROME (PMS)

Premenstrual Syndrome (PMS) involves symptoms that occur in relation to the menstrual cycle that can interfere with normal life activities. These symptoms can begin at ovulation and usually subside when menstruation begins. PMS affects most women during their childbearing years. It is thought that the change in hormone levels cause the symptoms, which can include mood swings, behavior changes, and/or physical discomfort such as bloating, constipation, diarrhea, headaches, migraines, and back pain.

How to Minister: (All commands done in Jesus' name.)

1. Lead them in a prayer of repentance for generational curses.
2. Command the hormones to be in balance.
3. Command the electrical and magnetic frequencies to be in harmony and balance.
4. Command the spirit of PMS to leave.
5. Command the ligaments to lengthen and pelvis to open to alleviate the pressure.

Prolapsed Uterus

Displacement of the uterus from its normal position in the lower abdomen into the vaginal canal is called a Prolapsed Uterus. Weakening of the lower abdominal muscles and ligaments associated with normal aging and a reduction in the female hormone estrogen allows the uterus to descend into the vaginal canal. Obesity, excessive coughing from lung/breathing problems, and chronic constipation can cause weakness in these muscles also.

How to Minister: (All commands done in Jesus' name.)

1. Command the muscles and ligaments around the uterus to strengthen, and the uterus to go back into place and function normally.
2. Command the pelvis to go into alignment.
3. Command the hormones to be in balance.
4. Lead them in a prayer for repentance, if necessary.

FIBROMYALGIA

Fibromyalgia is a condition characterized by widespread pain in joints, muscles, tendons, and other soft tissues. Other problems commonly associated with Fibromyalgia include fatigue, morning stiffness, sleep problems, headaches, numbness in hands and feet, depression, and anxiety. Fibromyalgia can develop alone or be associated with other conditions such as rheumatoid arthritis or systemic lupus.

Fibromyalgia pain can mimic the symptoms that occur with arthritis. The pain is described as aching, radiating, gnawing, shooting, or burning. Affected people tend to wake up complaining of body aches and stiffness. The cause is unknown.

How to Minister: (All commands done in Jesus' name.)

1. Cast out the spirit of Fibromyalgia.
2. Command the aches, pains, and stiffness to disappear.
3. Command the electrical and magnetic frequencies to be in harmony and balance.
4. Lead them in a prayer of repentance when necessary.
5. Lead them in a prayer to lay all stress, cares, worries, and fears on the altar of God.

FISSURE, RECTAL

This is a crack or a tear in the rectum that makes evacuation of the large bowel difficult or painful and may cause bleeding.

How to Minister: (All commands done in Jesus' name.)

1. Lay hands on the lower back and command the tissues to be healed and fissure to close.
2. Command the pain to go.

FLOATERS OR "WEBBING"

Floaters appear as specks "floating" in your vision. The specks, which are actually inside the eye, are bits of debris that appear and disappear without treatment. Described as spots or tiny threads, they are usually nothing to worry about; however, they can be a symptom of a tear in the retina of the eye.

How to Minister: (All commands done in Jesus' name.)

1. Lay hands on the eyes, commanding the blood and fluid in the eyes to be restored to normal function and all foreign substances to dissolve and go.
2. Command perfect sight to be restored.
3. If necessary, lead them in a prayer of repentance.

FLU (ALSO KNOWN AS INFLUENZA.)

The Flu is a contagious infection of the nose, throat, and lungs caused by the influenza virus. Symptoms include a high fever (over 102 degrees Fahrenheit), chills, sweats and severe fatigue. Some people have dizziness or vomiting. The virus can settle in the respiratory tract, producing additional symptoms of a cold, croup, sore throat, bronchitis, ear infection, or pneumonia. Cough and tiredness usually last for weeks after the rest of the symptoms are gone.

The Flu is spread from inhaling droplets from coughs or sneezes of an infected person, or touching a contaminated surface such as a faucet handle or phone and then touching your nose or mouth. Flu is airborne and very contagious with a short incubation period. Often infecting a community all at once, the Flu usually arrives in the winter months. Good hand washing is a key factor in stemming its spread.

How to Minister: (All commands done in Jesus' name.)

1. Rebuke the infection and curse the root of it.
2. Command the immune system to be strengthened and to function properly.
3. Command the electrical and magnetic frequencies to be in harmony and balance.
4. Command all pain and discomfort to disappear.
5. Command all affected tissues to be healed and function normally.

GALLSTONES

Gallstones are formed within the gallbladder, an organ that stores bile, a digestive juice made in the liver. If the concentration of the bile ingredients changes, Gallstones may form. Gallstones may be as small as a grain of sand or as large as an inch in diameter.

Gallstones often have no symptoms and are usually discovered incidentally by a routine X-ray. If a Gallstone passes into the small bile duct, it can trigger a very painful gall bladder attack. Surgical removal of the stones or gall bladder may be necessary.

How to Minister: (All commands done in Jesus' name.)

1. Lay your hand over the area of the gall bladder, commanding the stones to dissolve.
2. Command the gall bladder to be healed and function normally.

GANGLION CYST

This is a hard, tumorlike swelling filled with fluid; usually found on the wrist around a tendon or joint.

How to Minister: (All commands done in Jesus' name.)

1. Lay hands on the affected area, commanding the cyst to dissolve and fluid to reabsorb into the body.
2. Command the wrist structures, bones, muscles, and tendons to go back into normal position.
3. Command the joint lining to produce proper joint fluid and blood supply to be normal.
4. Command all pressure on the nerves to go back to normal.

138

GASTROESOPHAGEAL REFLUX DISEASE (GERD) (ALSO SEE HERNIA, HIATAL.)

Gastroesophageal Reflux Disease (GERD) is a condition in which food or liquid from the stomach backs up into the esophagus (the tube from the mouth to the stomach). This partially digested material usually contains stomach digestive acids and can irritate the esophagus causing heartburn, indigestion, and other symptoms such as middle chest discomfort.

This common condition often occurs without warning following a meal. In some people, the reflux is related to a problem with the band of muscle that closes off the esophagus from the stomach. If this opening does not close properly, food and liquid can move backward into the esophagus and cause the unpleasant symptoms.

How to Minister: (All commands done in Jesus' name.)

1. Command the muscles (sphincter) to function properly.
2. Lead them in the prayer to lay all cares, stress, and worries on the altar of God.
3. Lead them in a prayer of repentance for generational curses.

GINGIVITIS (SEE GUM DISEASE.)

GLAUCOMA

Glaucoma means there is increased fluid pressure inside the eye, which damages the optic nerve, limits vision, and can lead to total blindness.

Increased pressure occurs when the fluid within the eye does not drain properly. The increased pressure reduces the blood supply to the optic nerve, which carries visual information from the eye to the brain. The loss of blood supply causes the nerve cells to die and blind spots develop. Side vision is affected first, followed by frontal vision. Without treatment, glaucoma can eventually cause total blindness.

How to Minister: (All commands done in Jesus' name.)

1. Command the canals of the eyes to open and all pressure to normalize to allow fluid to flow normally.
2. Command any disease process or scar tissue to be healed and for the eyes to return to normal.
3. Command any damaged optic nerve cells to be healed and function normally.

GLUTTONY (See Addictions and Obesity.)

GOITER (Also see Thyroid.)

A Goiter is an enlargement of the thyroid, a gland located in the throat. A Goiter is NOT associated with inflammation or cancer. When the thyroid gland is not able to produce enough thyroid hormone to meet the body's requirements, the thyroid gland enlarges to overcome thyroid hormone deficiencies. Because iodine is vital to the formation of the thyroid hormone, iodized table salt in the U.S. prevents this nutritional deficiency and has decreased the incidence of Goiter.

How to Minister: (All commands done in Jesus' name.)

1. Lead them in a prayer of repentance for generational curses.
2. Lay hands on the Goiter and command it to dissolve.
3. Command the electrical and magnetic frequencies to be in harmony and balance.
4. Command a new thyroid gland that will function normally.

GOUT

Gout is a very painful disorder involving uric acid crystal deposits in the joints of the feet and legs. Patients with chronic Gout have repeated episodes of debilitating joint pain.

Even though the exact cause is not known, it is believed an excessive production of uric acid contributes to its development. The kidney's reduced ability to eliminate uric acid may also be a factor.

How to Minister: (All commands done in Jesus' name.)

1. Lay hands on the affected area and command the crystals to dissolve and tissues and bones to be healed.
2. Command the body to produce a normal amount of uric acid.
3. Lead them in a prayer of repentance for generational curses.

GUILLAIN-BARRÉ SYNDROME (ALSO KNOWN AS GBS.)

Guillain-Barré Syndrome is a rapidly disabling disorder caused by nerve inflammation, which causes progressive muscle weakness or paralysis. As the inflammation damages portions of the nerve cells, the creeping muscle weakness, paralysis, and sensory loss can move from the fingers and toes towards the trunk and then to the neck until total paralysis is present. Even though the damage can permanently affect nerve function, the condition can also spontaneously resolve the same way it appeared. In severe cases, the person "locked" within a nonresponsive body is conscious but cannot communicate. This syndrome is believed to be triggered by the body's autoimmune response to a viral or bacterial infection.

How to Minister: (All commands done in Jesus' name.)

1. Rebuke the infection and command the spirit to go.
2. Lay hands on the person and command the nervous system to be restored and function perfectly.
3. Command any other structures that have been damaged by the paralysis to become whole.
4. Lead them in a prayer of repentance if necessary.

GUM DISEASE (ALSO SEE PERIODONTITIS.)

Inadequate plaque removal from the teeth at the gum line can lead to inflamed gums also known as gingivitis. If the plaque is not removed with regular brushing of the teeth and dental appointments, it will harden into what is known as tartar. Tartar can lead to increased bleeding and a more advanced form of Gum Disease known as Periodontitis. Good mouth and tooth care can prevent Gum Disease.

How to Minister: (All commands done in Jesus' name.)
1. Rebuke the infection.
2. Lay hands on the jawbone, commanding the tissues of the mouth to be healed and function normally.
3. Lead them in a prayer of repentance for personal dental care, if necessary.
4. Lead them in a prayer of repentance to break word curses.

HAIR LOSS (SEE BALDNESS.)

HAMMER TOES

A Hammer Toe is a deformity of the toe in which the end of the toe is bent downward. Although a Hammer Toe usually affects the second toe, it may also affect the other toes. The affected toe appears claw-like. This condition may occur as a result of pressure from a bunion. Hammer Toes may be acquired by wearing ill-fitting shoes.

How to Minister: (All commands done in Jesus' name.)
1. Command all 26 bones in the foot to return to their normal position.
2. Command all tendons, ligaments, and muscles to return to their normal length and strength.

3. Grow out the legs and command the nerves to be restored in the spinal column.
4. Lead them in a prayer of repentance, if necessary.

HANDS (See Arms and Hands.)

HAY FEVER (See Allergies.)

HEADACHES

Headaches, Cluster

A Cluster Headache is a fairly common form of recurrent and often chronic headache. Cluster Headaches affect one side of the head and may be associated with tearing of the eyes and nasal congestion. They occur in clusters meaning they happen repeatedly every day at the same time for several weeks and then suddenly stop.

Although no specific cause has been found, smoking, alcohol use, glare, stress, or certain foods seem to trigger the attack.

How to Minister: (All commands done in Jesus' name.)

1. Command the histamines and the serotonin levels to be normal and in balance.
2. Lead them in a prayer of repentance when necessary.
3. Lead them in a prayer of repentance to break word curses.
4. Command the pain to go and blood to flow properly.
5. Lead them in a prayer to lay all cares, stress, and worries on the altar of God.
6. Command the blood to come into proper pH balance.

Headaches, Migraine

Migraine Headaches are a type of severely debilitating headache accompanied with symptoms such as nausea, vomiting, visual disturbances, or sensitivity to light and sound.

A Migraine Headache is caused by abnormal brain activity, which may be triggered by stress, foods, allergic reactions, bright lights, loud noises, certain odors or perfumes, smoking or exposure to smoke, alcohol, or caffeine. They can last from a few hours to several days. The best prevention is to identify the trigger and avoid it.

How to Minister: (All commands done in Jesus' name.)

1. Lead them in a prayer of repentance for generational curses.
2. Command the spirit of migraines to go.
3. Command the blood to flow properly to the brain.
4. Command the hormones to be in balance.
5. Lead them in a prayer of repentance to break word curses.
6. Command the pain to go.
7. Command the blood to come into proper pH balance.

HEADACHE, TENSION

A Headache is pain or discomfort in the head, scalp, or neck. Most people who suffer Headaches will improve by making lifestyle changes, learning ways to relax, and taking medications.

Tension Headaches are due to tight, contracted muscles in the shoulders, neck, scalp, and jaw. They are often related to such things as stress, depression, anxiety, overworking, not getting enough sleep, missing meals, using alcohol or street drugs, certain foods, or holding the head in one position for a long time (at a computer, microscope, or typewriter).

Tension Headaches tend to be on both sides of the head, often start at the back of the head and spread forward. The pain may feel dull or squeezing, like a tight band or vice. The shoulders, neck, or jaw may also feel tight and sore.

How to Minister: (All commands done in Jesus' name.)

1. Command the neck to come into alignment.

2. Command the blood to flow normally and spasms of the vessels to release.
3. Cast out the spirit of Headache, if necessary.
4. Lead them in a prayer of repentance, if necessary.
5. Lead them in a prayer of repentance for generational curses.
6. Lead them in a prayer to lay all cares, stress, and worries on the altar of God.
7. Command the blood to come into proper pH balance.

HEART

This includes any problem involving the heart.

HEART ARRHYTHMIA

An Arrhythmia is any disorder of the rhythm or heartbeat pattern. The heartbeat can be too slow, too fast, have extra beats, skip a beat, or otherwise beat irregularly.

There are numerous causes; however they are all related to an electrical dysfunction of the heart. Names of the more common specific rhythms are: Atrial Fibrillation, Bradycardia, PAT (Paroxysmal Atrial Tachycardia or PSVT), Ventricular Tachycardia, "skipped beats," Heart Block, or "Wolf-Parkinson-White" (WPW).

Causes of Arrhythmias range from Heart Attacks, metabolic imbalance, medication side effects, lack of oxygen, high blood pressure, congenital heart defects, abnormal heart valves, lung diseases, heart stimulants such as caffeine, tobacco, or alcohol, stress or viral infections, Coronary Artery Disease, to Arteriosclerosis.

Some people have no outward symptoms. Others complain about fast or slow heart beats (palpitations), fainting, light-headedness, dizziness, chest pain, shortness of breath, paleness, sweating, changes in the rate, rhythm, or pattern of the pulse.

Complications are serious and can be life-threatening: Angina (chest pain caused by lack of oxygen to the heart muscle), Heart Attack, Heart Failure, Stroke, and sudden death.

HEART ATTACK

A Heart Attack (also called myocardial infarction or MI) occurs when an area of heart muscle dies or is permanently damaged because of an inadequate supply of oxygen to that area.

Most Heart Attacks are caused by a blood clot that blocks one of the coronary arteries (the blood vessels that bring blood and oxygen to the heart muscle). The plaque buildup inside the wall of a coronary artery (arteriosclerosis) triggers the formation of a blood clot, which, in turn, interrupts the flow of blood and supply of oxygen to the heart muscle causing the death of heart cells in that area. The damaged heart muscle loses its ability to pump blood to the body and lungs.

As the damage increases, Congestive Heart Failure can develop. Prompt treatment with medications or surgery can prevent death.

HEART, CONGENITAL HEART DEFECTS

This refers to any defect of the heart present at birth. Heart Defects involve holes in the heart muscle that either should not be there or that should have closed after birth but didn't. Other defects involving the heart valves can cause numerous complications and are very often life-threatening to a baby. They need a new heart.

HEART DISEASE

Heart Disease includes any disorder that affects the heart's ability to function normally. The most common cause of Heart Disease is narrowing or blockage of the coronary arteries, which supply blood to the heart itself. This happens slowly over time.

Some Heart Disease can be present at birth (congenital heart diseases).

Other causes include: hypertension, abnormal function of the heart valves, abnormal electrical rhythm of the heart, or weakening of the heart's pumping function caused by blockage of coronary arteries, infection, or toxins.

HEART FAILURE

Also called Congestive Heart Failure, Heart Failure is a disorder in which the heart loses its ability to pump blood efficiently throughout the body. The heart is unable to supply the vital organs of the body with enough blood to meet the body's demands for necessary nutrition and oxygen. Fluid then backs up into the lungs and causes breathing problems. It can also back up into other areas of the body causing problems with swelling (edema) of the lower legs.

The term "Heart Failure" should not be confused with cardiac arrest, a situation in which the heart actually stops beating. Heart Failure is almost always a chronic, long-term condition, although it can sometimes develop suddenly. Congestive Heart Failure can usually be controlled by medications and diet.

HEART, VALVULAR HEART DISEASE

Valvular Heart Disease refers to any condition of the four heart valves: the mitral valve, aortic valve, tricuspid valve, and pulmonic valve. Such conditions include valvular regurgitation (the valve closes improperly allowing leakage of blood) and stenosis (narrowing or stiffening of a valve restricting the flow of blood). Surgical replacement is often necessary. These problems can be caused by infection or other disease processes. Numerous other body functions are affected by Valvular Heart Disease. It can lead to Congestive Heart Failure, Arrhythmias, Endocarditis (inflammation of the heart tissue), Pulmonary Edema, and cardiac arrest (heart stops beating leading to death).

How to Minister: (All commands done in Jesus' name.)

1. Command a creative miracle or "a new heart" into the body.
2. Cast out the spirit of death.
3. Command the electrical and magnetic frequencies to be in harmony and balance.
4. Command all the excess fluid to leave the body and breathing be normal.
5. Lead them in a prayer of repentance for lifestyle or diet, if necessary.
6. Lead them in a prayer of repentance for generational curses.
7. Command other body parts that have been affected by the heart disease/damage to be healed and function normally.
8. Lead them in a prayer of repentance to break word curses.

HEMORRHOIDS

Hemorrhoids are painful, swollen veins in the lower portion of the rectum or anus. Hemorrhoids result from increased pressure that causes the veins to bulge and expand, making them painful, particularly when sitting or passing a stool.

This condition is very common during pregnancy and after childbirth due to the excess pressure caused by carrying a child; however, the most common cause is straining during bowel movements. Hemorrhoids may result from constipation, sitting for long periods of time, and infections to the area. Topical preparations may help control the discomfort. Surgical removal is another option.

How to Minister: (All commands done in Jesus' name.)

1. Place hands on the lower back and command the hemorrhoids to be healed.
2. Command the blood vessels to shrink to normal size and function.
3. Rebuke pain.
4. Adjust the pelvis into proper alignment.
5. Command the nerves and muscles to be relaxed and normal.
6. Lead them in a prayer of repentance for diet, if necessary.

HEPATITIS C

Hepatitis C is an inflammation of the liver caused by the Hepatitis C virus. Hepatitis C is often detected during blood tests for a routine physical or other medical procedure. If the infection has been present for many years, the liver may be permanently scarred—a condition called cirrhosis. In many cases, there may be no symptoms of the disease until cirrhosis has developed.

Hepatitis C is a blood borne virus and is often referred to as the "silent epidemic" because symptoms may not appear for years after a person is infected.

How to Minister: (All commands done in Jesus' name.)

1. Curse the virus and command the spirit to leave.
2. Lead them in a prayer of repentance, if necessary.
3. Command a creative miracle of a new liver if it is damaged.
4. Command the electrical and magnetic frequencies to be in harmony and in balance.

HERNIA

A hernia occurs when parts of an organ (usually the intestines) protrudes through a weak area in the muscular wall that holds the abdominal organs in place. It appears as a soft swelling in the area. Usually, there is no obvious cause of a hernia, although they are sometimes associated with heavy lifting.

There are several types of hernias, based on where they occur. The most common types involving the bowel include: Inguinal hernia (a bulge in the groin or scrotum), Femoral hernia (a bulge in the upper thigh), Incisional hernia (bulge through a scar after abdominal surgery), and Umbilical hernia (a bulge around the belly button or umbilicus).

Hernias rarely go away without treatment. If the bulging abdominal tissue becomes trapped and can no longer be pushed back into the abdominal cavity, the decreased blood supply to the involved intestine can lead to tissue death. If not relieved, the person may develop signs and symptoms of bowel obstruction which include abdominal cramps, bloating, and vomiting. Emergency surgery may be required.

Hiatal Hernia—This protrusion of the stomach above the diaphragm leads to pain, indigestion, and swallowing difficulties. Food can get trapped in this pocket and cause severe pain as well as spontaneous vomiting. Symptoms may be similar to GERDS.

How to Minister: (All commands done in Jesus' name.)

1. Grow out the arms.
2. Grow out the legs.
3. Command the hernia to disappear; muscles, nerves, tendons, ligaments, and tissues to be healed and restored to proper alignment, strength, and function.
4. Command the pelvis to come into proper alignment.
5. Lead them in a prayer of repentance for generational curses.

HERPES

Herpes is a viral infection affecting various parts of the body.

HERPES SIMPLEX HSV 1 (COLD SORE)

Herpes Simplex is an infection caused by the Herpes Simplex virus 1 and is commonly called a Cold Sore. It primarily affects the areas of the lips, mouth, and face often causing Cold Sores and fever blisters inside the mouth. This Herpes virus is transmitted by contact with infected saliva.

How to Minister: (All commands done in Jesus' name.)

1. Curse the root of the virus and command the spirit to leave.
2. Lead them in a prayer of repentance for generational curses.
3. Command healing in the affected areas and all affected tissues to be restored.
4. Command the electrical and magnetic frequencies to be in harmony and balance.

HERPES SIMPLEX HSV-2 (GENITAL HERPES)

Genital Herpes is a sexually transmitted viral infection that is characterized by repeated eruptions of small, painful ulcers, blisters, or sores on the genitals or adjacent skin.

How to Minister: (All commands done in Jesus' name.)

1. Curse the root of the virus and command the spirit to leave.
2. Lead them in a prayer of repentance for generational curses.
3. Command healing in the affected areas and all affected tissues to be restored.
4. Command the electrical and magnetic frequencies to be in harmony and balance.
5. Lead them in a prayer of repentance, if necessary.

6. Command the immune system to be strong and function properly.

HERPES ZOSTER (ALSO KNOWN AS SHINGLES.)

Herpes Zoster is a localized infection caused by the varicella-zoster virus, which causes a very painful, blistering rash. Herpes Zoster, or Shingles, is caused by the same virus that causes chickenpox. After an episode of chickenpox, the virus becomes dormant, hiding along nerve pathways in the body. Herpes Zoster develops when the virus re-emerges years later. The fluid within the blisters can cause chickenpox in a susceptible person.

How to Minister: (All commands done in Jesus' name.)

1. Curse the root of the virus and command the spirit to leave.
2. Lead them in a prayer of repentance for generational curses.
3. Command healing in the affected areas and all affected tissues to be restored.
4. Command the electrical and magnetic frequencies to be in harmony and balance.
5. Lead them in a prayer to lay all their cares, worries, and stress on the altar of God.
6. Command the immune system to be strong and function properly.

HICCUPS (ALSO KNOWN AS HICCOUGHS.)

A Hiccup is a sudden involuntary spasm of the diaphragm muscle at the base of the lungs. The spasm is followed by rapid closure of the vocal cords in the throat which produces a distinctive sound as air is stopped from entry into the lungs.

Hiccups often start for no apparent reason and usually disappear after a few minutes. Rarely, Hiccups can persist for days, weeks, or months. Hiccups are common and normal in newborns and infants.

How to Minister: (All commands done in Jesus' name.)

1. Command the diaphragm to be at peace and the spasms to stop.

HIGH CHOLESTEROL (See Cholesterol, High.)

HIV/AIDS (See AIDS.)

HOMOSEXUALITY/LESBIANISM

This term identifies individuals who prefer intimate relationships with others of the same sex; the term homosexual refers to males, lesbian refers to females. The individual must want to be free from the desire before they can be delivered and healed from this condition.

How to Minister: (All commands done in Jesus' name.)

1. Lead them in a prayer of repentance of idolatry.
2. Have them repent of sexual sins, if necessary (no details need to be spoken).
3. Lead them in the prayer to break ungodly covenants.
4. Cast out the spirit of homosexuality/lesbianism.
5. Lead them in a prayer of repentance to break word curses.
6. Minister to the emptiness in their heart. Speak peace to them.

HUNTINGTON'S CHOREA

An inherited disease, Huntington's Chorea is characterized by involuntary, abnormal, incessant jerky body movements, emotional disturbances, and dementia. Huntington's disease exhibits progressive wasting of nerve cells in the brain with loss of mental function, including personality changes, and loss of cognitive functions such as judgment and speech. There is no cure.

How to Minister: (All commands done in Jesus' name.)

1. Lead them in a prayer of repentance for generational curses.
2. Cast out the spirit of Huntington's disease.
3. Command all the chromosomes to become normal.
4. Command any affected organs to be restored and to function normally.

HYPERLIPIDEMIA (SEE CHOLESTEROL, HIGH.)

HYPERTENSION (ALSO CALLED HIGH BLOOD PRESSURE OR HTN. SEE BLOOD PRESSURE PROBLEMS.)

HYPOGLYCEMIA (LOW BLOOD SUGAR.)

Hypoglycemia occurs when the body's blood sugar, or glucose, is abnormally low. It can develop when the body's glucose is burned up too rapidly, when glucose is released into the bloodstream too slowly, or when excessive insulin is present in the bloodstream. Insulin is a hormone that reduces blood glucose and is produced by the pancreas in response to increased glucose levels in the blood. The term insulin shock describes severe Hypoglycemia that results in unconsciousness. If blood sugar levels continue to fall, seizures and death can follow. Hypoglycemia is common with Diabetics if they do not eat enough food after taking their antidiabetic medication (by mouth or injection).

How to Minister: (All commands done in Jesus' name.)

1. Lead them in a prayer of repentance for generational curses.
2. Command the spirit of hypoglycemia to go.
3. Command a new pancreas to maintain blood sugar at normal levels.

IBS (SEE IRRITABLE BOWEL SYNDROME.)

IMMUNE SYSTEM (SEE CHAPTER 12 FOR DETAILS ON THE IMMUNE SYSTEM FUNCTIONS AND PROBLEMS.)

How to Minister: (All commands done in Jesus' name.)

1. Command the immune system to be restored completely.
2. Command it to stop all disease and viruses from infecting the body.
3. Command the electrical and magnetic frequencies to be in harmony and balance.
4. Lead them in a prayer of repentance, if necessary.

INCONTINENCE

Urinary Incontinence is the inability to control the passage of urine out of the body. This can range from an occasional leakage of urine, to a complete inability to hold any urine at any time. There are two main types of urinary incontinence.

Stress incontinence occurs during certain activities like coughing, sneezing, laughing, or exercise.

Urge incontinence involves a strong, sudden need to urinate followed by the involuntary loss of urine.

Incontinence is most common among the elderly. Loss of control can be caused by loss of function following neurological problems such as spinal injury, brain injury, back surgery, or stroke. It is common in women after birthing several children or, with men, following prostate surgery.

Bowel Incontinence is the inability to control passage of stool. This can range from an occasional leakage of stool to a complete loss of control of any bowel movements. This loss of control can be caused by loss of function following spinal injury, brain injury, back surgery or a stroke. Infection, irritability of the colon, and diseases such as Crohn's also can contribute to this problem. It is common with people who have limited mental capacity.

How to Minister: (All commands done in Jesus' name.)

1. Command the nerves and muscles in the effected area to operate properly.
2. Command any irritation/infection to leave.
3. Lead them in prayer to lay stress, cares, and worries on the altar of God.

INCURABLE DISEASES

This includes any disease for which doctors cannot find a cure.

How to Minister: (All commands done in Jesus' name.)

1. Cast out the spirit of whatever disease is involved.
2. Speak healing or new parts into the body.
3. Lead them in a prayer of repentance, if necessary.
4. Lead them in a prayer of repentance to break word curses.

INDIGESTION (See GERDS.)

INFECTION

Any one of numerous organisms (such as bacteria, viruses, fungi, or parasites) can cause infection within the body. Some bacteria are normal within the body as part of the digestive process. However, if this bacteria is relocated to another area of the body, it becomes an infection and can cause serious problems. For example, bacteria from the colon can contaminate the urinary tract where it causes a urinary tract infection.

How to Minister: (All commands done in Jesus' name.)

1. Rebuke the infection.
2. Command the body to be healed and restored to normal condition and function.

3. Command the immune system to work properly.
4. Lead them in a prayer of repentance, if necessary.
5. Command the electrical and magnetic frequencies to be in harmony and balance.

INFERTILITY

Infertility is the inability to achieve a pregnancy. Causes of Infertility include a wide range of physical as well as emotional factors. The contributing factors can be from either or both partners. There also may be no cause that can be identified.

How to Minister: (All commands done in Jesus' name.)

**Before praying, confirm they are married.
1. Command the pelvis to be adjusted.
2. Command the reproductive system to function normally.
3. Lead them in a prayer of repentance for generational curses.
4. Lead them in a prayer for ungodly covenants.
5. Say, "Father, Your Word says the womb of Your children shall not be barren, and You will make the barren woman the joyful mother of many children."

INFLUENZA (SEE FLU.)

INSOMNIA (SEE SLEEP DISORDERS.)

IRRITABLE BOWEL SYNDROME (IBS)

Irritable Bowel Syndrome is a disorder of the lower intestinal tract. Often worsened by emotional stress, this condition involves hypersensitivity to pain in the abdomen combined with excessive gas, bloating, and alternating bouts of diarrhea and constipation.

How to Minister: (All commands done in Jesus' name.)

1. Command the intestines to be at peace and all irritation to leave.
2. Command the intestines to function normally.
3. Lead them in a prayer of repentance, if necessary.
4. Lead them in prayer to lay all stress, cares, and worries on the altar of God.

JAW (Dislocated, Fractured, or Broken Jaw.)

A broken or dislocated Jaw is a facial injury that results in the jawbone breaking or moving out of position. The jawbone is the movable bone at the bottom of the face.

How to Minister: (All commands done in Jesus' name.)

1. Command the joint with its cartilage, ligaments, tendons, and tissues to be healed and work normally.
2. If a bone is out of joint, command it to go back into the socket and stay there.
3. Lead them in a prayer for repentance to break word curses.
4. Command the neck to come into alignment.

KELOIDS (See Scars, Keloids, and Adhesions.)

KIDNEY DISEASE

Kidney Disease includes any disease or disorder that affects the function of the kidneys.

How to Minister: (All commands done in Jesus' name.)

1. Command a new pair of kidneys to operate and function normally.
2. Command healing for underlying causes such as disease, high blood pressure, diabetes, or infections.

3. Command any pain or discomfort to leave.
4. Command the pelvis to come into alignment.

KIDNEY STONES

Kidney Stones form within the center of the kidney. As urine produced by the kidney passes from the kidney to the bladder, it flushes the stones out of the body. If these stones increase in size, passage from the kidney to the bladder can be both difficult and extremely painful. These abnormal stones can cause damage to all areas of the urinary system.

How to Minister: (All commands done in Jesus' name.)

1. Lead them in a prayer of repentance for generational curses.
2. Command the stones to dissolve and pass out of the body.
3. Command the pain to go.
4. Command the kidneys and all damaged tissues to be healed and restored to normal function.

KIDNEY FAILURE (ALSO CALLED END-STAGE RENAL DISEASE OR RENAL FAILURE.)

Kidney Failure indicates the kidneys are unable to function normally. Damaged kidneys cannot filter waste liquid, waste products, concentrate urine, or conserve substances vital to the health of the total body. Diabetes, hypertension, toxins, medications, and severe illnesses can cause renal failure and ESRD (End-Stage Renal Disease).

Numerous serious complications result from this condition including Congestive Heart Failure and death. Dialysis is the immediate treatment with kidney transplant as a possible necessity to maintain life.

How to Minister: (All commands done in Jesus' name.)

1. Command a creative miracle or "new kidneys" into the body.

2. Cast out the spirit of death.
3. Command the electrical and magnetic frequencies to be in harmony and balance.
4. Command all the excess fluid and impurities to leave the body.
5. Lead them in a prayer of repentance for generational curses.
6. Command other body parts that have been affected by the kidney disease/damage to be healed and function normally.

KNEECAP PROBLEMS

These problems can be caused by disease, traumatic injury, or developmental abnormalities. A dislocated Kneecap means the triangular bone covering the knee moves or slides out of place usually towards the outside of the leg. It is usually a result of a sudden direction change while running putting the knee under stress. Dislocation may also occur as a direct result of injury such as a fall.

How to Minister: (All commands done in Jesus' name.)

1. Where arthritis is involved, cast out the spirit of arthritis.
2. Lay hands on the affected area, commanding all the tendons, ligaments, muscles, cartilage, and tissues to be healed; command the blood and fluid to lubricate the area to be restored.
3. Command a new Kneecap, if needed.
4. Lead them in a prayer of repentance for generational curses.

KNOCK-KNEED

When a person is Knock-kneed, the lower legs are at an outward angle with the knees touching and the ankles separated.

Young children develop a slight knock-kneed stance that is part of normal development. By puberty, most children can stand normally with the knees and ankles touching.

How to Minister: (All commands done in Jesus' name.)

1. Commanding the pelvic bone to rotate outward, do the pelvis adjustment.
2. Grow out the legs.
3. Command the legs and knees to straighten.
4. Lead them in a prayer of repentance for generational curses.

LARYNGITIS

Laryngitis is an inflammation of the voice box due to over-use, irritation, or infection. Vocal cords located inside the larynx normally open and close smoothly as words or sounds are produced. Inflamed, infected, or irritated vocal cords swell, causing distortion of the sounds or hoarseness of the voice. Long lasting hoarseness or Laryngitis can indicate a more serious underlying problem.

Laryngitis can be caused by a sore or dry throat, a viral infection, a bacterial infection, a cold, flu, or pneumonia. Common causes of chronic Laryngitis include persistent irritation from excessive alcohol, heavy smoking, or reflux of stomach acid into the esophagus and throat. Overuse of your voice, by speaking too much, speaking too loudly, shouting or singing over an extended period of time can also contribute to the development of Laryngitis.

How to Minister: (All commands done in Jesus' name.)

1. Curse the root of any viral or bacteria infection.
2. Lead them in a prayer of repentance to break word curses.
3. Command the inflammation or irritation to go.
4. Command all the tissues of the throat to function normally and be totally healed.

LAZY EYE (See Amblyopia.)

LEUKEMIA

Leukemia is a type of blood cancer. Immature blood cells multiply uncontrolled in the bone marrow and take the place of normal blood. This leads to infection (not enough white cells to destroy bacteria), anemia (not enough red blood cells to carry oxygen to the body), abnormal bleeding (decreased platelets, which aid in clotting), other malfunctions of the body and death. If left untreated, acute Leukemia can be fatal in a matter of weeks or months, depending on the patient's situation.

How to Minister: (All commands done in Jesus' name.)

1. Curse the root of the Leukemia and cast out the spirit of death.
2. Lead them in a prayer of repentance for generational curses.
3. Lead them in a prayer of repentance for bitterness or unforgiveness, if necessary.
4. Command electrical and magnetic frequencies to be in harmony and balance.
5. Curse any prions and command them to dissolve and be discarded.
6. Command the marrow to make the proper amount of white blood cells.

LIGAMENTS (Torn or Damaged)

Ligaments connect bones or cartilage at a joint or support an organ, muscle, or other body part. Since ligaments are located throughout the body, this type of injury can occur anywhere; however, the most common sites of injury are the joints of the shoulders, arms, legs, hips, or back. This condition is usually caused by twisting, excessive stretching, or some form of trauma.

How to Minister: (All commands done in Jesus' name.)

1. Rebuke any infection or inflammation.
2. Do the adjustment necessary: Grow out the arms or legs; adjust the neck, back, and/or pelvis.
3. Lead them in a prayer of repentance, if necessary.
4. Command the ligaments to be healed and restored to normal function.

LIGHTHEADEDNESS (See Dizziness, Vertigo.)

LOU GEHRIG'S DISEASE (See Amyotrophic Lateral Sclerosis. Also called ALS.)

LUMPS (Also see Tumors)

Abnormal growths found in or on the body.

How to Minister: (All commands done in Jesus' name.)

1. Curse the core, root, and cause of the lump.
2. Lay hands on the affected area commanding the lump to dissolve and disappear.
3. Command all tissues to be healed and restored to normal function.
4. Lead them in a prayer of repentance, if necessary.

LUNG DISEASE (Also see Asthma, Emphysema, COPD, Pleurisy, Sarcoidosis, and Pneumonia)

Lung Disease is any disease or disorder where lung function is impaired. Most Lung Diseases actually involve a combination of breathing problems such as Emphysema, which involves both airflow obstruction and oxygenation problems.

How to Minister: (All commands done in Jesus' name.)

1. Command new lungs and new organs that may have been damaged.

2. Command the air sacs to open, excess fluid to dry up, or whatever symptoms that need healing.
3. Lead them in a prayer for repentance, if necessary.
4. Command the electrical and magnetic frequencies to be in harmony and balance.

LUPUS ERYTHEMATOSUS

Lupus Erythematosus (SLE) is a chronic, inflammatory autoimmune disorder. It may affect many organ systems including the skin, joints, and internal organs.

Normally, the immune system functions as the body's defense against infection or bacteria. In SLE and other autoimmune diseases, the immune system attacks normal body tissues causing numerous malfunctions and symptoms in many parts of the body.

How to Minister: (All commands done in Jesus' name.)
1. Cast out the spirit of Lupus.
2. Command the immune system and all affected organs to be healed and to function normally.
3. Lead them in a prayer of repentance for generational curses.
4. Command the electrical and magnetic frequencies to be in harmony and in balance.

LYMPHEDEMA (See Edema.)

MACULAR DEGENERATION

Macular Degeneration causes decreased and possible loss of central vision. The macula is the central part of the retina that allows the eye to see fine details at the center of the field of vision.

Even though central vision is lost, the peripheral fields are maintained. The ability to read and drive may be gone; however, the disease does not lead to complete blindness.

How to Minister: (All commands done in Jesus' name.)

1. Lay hands over the eyes. Speak a creative miracle and command a new retina and the macula to be totally restored.
2. Lead in the prayer of repentance for generational curses.
3. Command the blood filters in the eyes to work properly.

MARRIAGE PROBLEMS

Marriage problems include but are not limited to a lack of sexual intimacy, exploding temper during an argument, uncontrolled emotions, being selfish, dishonesty, excessive teasing, lack of respect for their spouse, inattentiveness to their spouse, not listening to their spouse, infidelity, breakdown in communication, abuse, and/or financial difficulties.

How to Minister: (All commands done in Jesus' name.)

1. Have each one cancel the debt the other owes them.
2. Lead them in prayers of forgiveness.
3. Have each one offer their heart without conditions.
4. Instruct them to seek godly counsel from Christians with successful marriages.

MASTITIS (See Cystic Disease.)

MENIERE'S DISEASE (Also see Dizziness and Vertigo.)

Meniere's Disease is a disorder of the inner ear affecting balance and hearing, characterized by vertigo, dizziness, fluctuating hearing loss, or fullness in one or both ears, and tinnitus (noises such as buzzing or ringing in the ears).

The inner ear controls balance and the sense of body position. Meniere's Disease involves swelling of a portion of the inner ear. The exact cause of Meniere's Disease is unknown. In some cases, it may be related to middle ear infection, head injury, viral illness, respiratory infection, stress, fatigue, use of prescription or nonprescription drugs including aspirin, allergies, smoking, or alcohol use. There may be genetic risk factors as well.

How to Minister: (All commands done in Jesus' name.)

1. Cast out the spirit of Meniere's Disease.
2. Command the inner ear to be healed, the nerves and blood flow to the inner ear to be normal, normal hearing to return, and all dizziness to stop.

MENOPAUSE (See Female Problems.)

MENSTRUAL PAIN (See Female Problems.)

MENTAL ILLNESS (Also see Depression, Schizophrenia, Bipolar Disorder, and Psychosis.)

Mental Illness refers to any mental disorder that causes abnormal behavior (including but not limited to schizophrenia, dementia, major depression, and bipolar disorder) accompanied by significant functional impairment, disruption of normal activities of daily living, periodic hospitalizations to total disability. Research indicates that many of these conditions are caused by a combination of genetic, biological, psychological, and environmental factors. With proper treatment, people with these problems can still lead normal lives.

How to Minister: (All commands done in Jesus' name.)

1. Command the spirit of Mental Illness to come out.
2. Lead them in a prayer of repentance for generational curses.
3. If caused by an accident or injury, command new nerves and a new brain that will function perfectly.

166

4. If a chemical disorder, command the production of proper chemicals in normal amounts.
5. Curse any prions. Command them to be dissolved.
6. Command the electrical and magnetic frequencies to be in harmony and balance.

MIGRAINE (SEE HEADACHES.)

MONGOLISM (SEE DOWN SYNDROME.)

MONONUCLEOSIS (ALSO CALLED "KISSING DISEASE".)

Infectious Mononucleosis (mono) or glandular fever is often called the "kissing disease" because kissing can spread the Epstein-Barr virus that causes this disease, although coughing, sneezing, or sharing a glass or cup more often transmits the virus.

Symptoms include a severe sore throat, painful swallowing, fatigue, weakness, swollen lymph nodes, headache, fever, and a tender spleen. The disease usually is not very serious, although the virus remains in the body for life and the lasting effects of exhaustion can remain for months.

Mononucleosis can result in complications such as Anemia, inflammation of the heart, meningitis, Encephalitis, Seizures, Bell's palsy, Guillain-Barré Syndrome, and swollen tonsils, which can cause problems breathing.

How to Minister: (All commands done in Jesus' name.)

1. Command the virus and all the symptoms to go.
2. Command the immune system to function normally.
3. Command the electrical and magnetic frequencies to be in harmony and balance.
4. Command all body systems to return to normal including all circulation, nerve function, muscle strength, and endurance levels.

MOTION SICKNESS

Motion Sickness (also known as car sickness, sea sickness, or air sickness) usually occurs when riding in a car, boat, airplane, or any other passive locomotion. Motion Sickness can also be caused by motion in the visual surroundings while standing still (viewing a large screen movie that contains significant motion). It can strike suddenly, progressing from a feeling of restlessness to a cold sweat, dizziness, vertigo, and then vomiting.

How to Minister: (All commands done in Jesus' name.)

1. Lead them in a prayer of repentance for generational curses.
2. Command the inner ear to adjust to movements.
3. Command the nerve messages from the eyes and ears to be in balance.
4. Command the dizziness and/or vertigo to go.

MULTIPLE SCLEROSIS (MS)

Multiple Sclerosis is a disorder of the brain and spinal cord caused by damage to the outer covering of nerve cells. The decreased nerve functioning can lead to a variety of symptoms including extreme weakness with increasing loss of control of muscles and other bodily functions.

Episodes progressively attack the nervous system with inflammation that destroys the covering of the nerve cells in that area leaving multiple areas of scar tissue (called sclerosis). This results in slowing or blocking of the transmission of nerve impulses in that area, leading to the symptoms of MS. This progressive disease leads to total disability and dependence for all activities of daily living.

How to Minister: (All commands done in Jesus' name.)

1. Cast out the spirit of Multiple Sclerosis.
2. Lead them in a prayer of repentance for generational curses.

3. Command the immune system to react normally.
4. Command healing and normal function to all parts of the body that have been affected by the disease.
5. Command the electrical and magnetic frequencies to be in harmony and balance.

MUSCULAR DYSTROPHY (MD)

Muscular Dystrophy is a genetic disorder characterized by progressive wasting and weakening of muscles leading to total disability and loss of function of most bodily functions as well as the necessity of mechanical ventilation support for breathing.

How to Minister: (All commands done in Jesus' name.)

1. Cast out the spirit of Muscular Dystrophy.
2. Lead them in a prayer of repentance for generational curses.
3. Command the electrical and magnetic frequencies to be in harmony and balance.
4. Command all the muscles to return to normal and all damaged affected tissues to be healed.

MYASTHENIA GRAVIS

Myasthenia Gravis is a disorder of the nerves and muscles of the body caused by an abnormal autoimmune response. It exhibits variable weakness of voluntary muscles that often improves with rest and worsens with activity. In Myasthenia Gravis, the information from the brain does not adequately reach the muscles through the nerve pathways. The precipitating cause is unknown. In some cases, Myasthenia Gravis may be associated with tumors of an organ of the immune system.

How to Minister: (All commands done in Jesus' name.)

1. Cast out the spirit of Myasthenia Gravis.

2. Command the nerve receptors on the muscles to be healed and function normally.
3. Command the immune system to be restored and function normally.
4. Command the electrical and magnetic frequencies to be in harmony and balance.

MYOPIA (See Nearsightedness.)

NAIL BITING

Onychophagia is the clinical term for chronic nail biting. This behavior (habit) often starts in childhood and can be exacerbated by stress.

How to Minister: (All commands done in Jesus' name.)

1. Lead them in a prayer of repentance for generational curses.
2. Lead in a prayer to lay all cares, stress, and worries on the altar of God.
3. Instruct them to break the habit by repeating (each time they want to start biting their nails) "I will not participate in onychophagia." (on-i-ko-FAY-jee-uh)

NARCOLEPSY (See Sleep Disorders.)

NASAL CONGESTION (See Nose.)

NEARSIGHTEDNESS (Also known as Myopia.)

Nearsightedness is a vision problem that makes distant objects appear blurred while close objects are seen clearly. As a result, someone with Myopia tends to squint when viewing far away objects. This condition is often identified in a school-aged child or teenager and requires frequent changes in glasses or contact lenses.

How to Minister: (All commands done in Jesus' name.)

1. Lay hands on the eyes, commanding the lens, nerves, ligaments, and muscles to be adjusted and work properly.
2. Command perfect sight to be restored.
3. Lead them in a prayer of repentance, if necessary.

NECK PAIN

Neck Pain may originate from any of the muscles, nerves, spinal vertebrae, and the cushioning discs in between the vertebrae. Neck pain may also come from regions near the neck like the shoulder, jaw, head, and upper arms.

Many people describe this as having a "stiff neck." If Neck Pain involves nerves (for example, a significant muscle spasm or a slipped disc pressing on a nerve), numbness, tingling, or weakness in the arm, hand, or elsewhere may be felt also.

Common Neck Pain is from muscle strain or tension from everyday activities such as bending over a desk, poor posture while watching TV or reading, working at a computer monitor positioned too high or too low, sleeping in an uncomfortable position, or twisting and turning the neck in a jarring manner during exercise.

Traumatic accidents or falls can also cause severe neck injuries such as broken necks, whiplash, blood vessel damage, and even paralysis. Other causes include a herniated disc, Fibromyalgia (pain syndrome throughout the body), and Arthritis.

How to Minister: (All commands done in Jesus' name.)

1. Command the neck to come into alignment.
2. Command vertebrae, discs, muscles, ligaments, nerves, and tendons to be healed and to go back into normal position.
3. Lead them in a prayer to lay cares, worries, and stress on the altar of God.

NERVOUSNESS (See Fear and Anxiety.)

NIGHTMARES

A nightmare is a dream that brings out feelings of strong, inescapable fear, terror, distress, or extreme anxiety. They typically occur in the early morning hours and usually awaken the sleeper who can recall the details of the dream. Nightmares tend to be more common among children and decrease in frequency toward adulthood. They can stem from previous severe trauma or abuse.

How to Minister: (All commands done in Jesus' name.)

1. Lead them in a prayer of repentance for generational curses.
2. Lead them in a prayer of repentance for demonic entertainment, TV, and/or movies.
3. Speak peace to them.

NOSE PROBLEMS (Also see Colds, Allergies, Flu, and Sinus Problems.)

This includes all problems involving the nose including nasal or sinus congestion or a runny nose. Congestion develops when the membranes lining the nose become swollen from inflamed blood vessels. Congestion is often a symptom of colds, allergies, sinus infections, or the flu. Overuse of some nasal sprays or drops can also lead to congestion.

How to Minister: (All commands done in Jesus' name.)

1. Lead them in a prayer of repentance for generational curses.
2. Curse the root cause (allergies, chronic infection, etc.) and command healing of the effected areas.
3. Command the nasal passages to remain open and to drain properly.
4. Command the immune system to work properly.

NOSE INJURY

The most common facial fracture is a break in the bone over the bridge of the nose. It usually results from a blunt injury and is often associated with other facial fractures. The characteristic bruising around the eyes and nose usually disappears after two weeks.

Sometimes, as a result of an injury, the wall dividing the nostrils can separate causing the same symptoms as a fractured nose. A deviated septum makes one air passage larger than the other and can cause problems with normal breathing through the nose. Nose and neck problems are often seen together after a traumatic injury.

How to Minister: (All commands done in Jesus' name.)

1. Lay your finger on the nose and gently run it down the crest, commanding it to be straight, structures to be regenerated, and to function normally.
2. Do the neck adjustment.
3. Cast out the spirit of trauma, if necessary.

RHINITIS

The term Rhinitis covers infections, allergies, and other disorders of the nose. The mucous membranes of the nose become infected, inflamed, or irritated and produce a discharge, congestion, and swelling of the nasal tissues. Symptoms include red itchy eyes, difficulty breathing and sleeping, a scratchy throat, coughing, runny nose, headaches or Post Nasal Drip (the excess liquid or mucus drains down the back of the throat).

The most widespread form of infectious Rhinitis is the common cold. Another common cause includes environmental allergies such as hay fever.

How to Minister: (All commands done in Jesus' name.)

1. Curse the root of the infection or inflammation and command it to go.
2. Command healing to the lining of the nose and sinuses and for the mucus to drain normally.
3. Lead them in a prayer for repentance, if necessary.

NUMBNESS

Numbness and tingling are abnormal sensations that most often affect the hands, feet, arms, or legs. This is often a symptom of an underlying problem.

There are many possible causes that usually include abnormal circulation or damaged nerves to an area of the body. A neck injury may cause numbness anywhere along the arm or hand. Similarly, a low back (spine) injury can cause sciatica—a sensation of numbness or tingling down the back of a leg.

Poor blood supply from atherosclerosis can precipitate pain, numbness, and tingling in the legs. This may be diagnosed by a doctor as PVD (Peripheral Vascular Disease), PAD (Peripheral Arterial Disease), or Neuropathy. Pressure on the spinal nerves or damage to the brain (stroke or head injury) can cause numbness anywhere in the body. Carpal Tunnel Syndrome causes numbness or tingling in your wrist, fingers, hand, or forearm.

Permanent numbness is found with paralysis (quadriplegia—all four extremities; or paraplegia—legs) where the spinal cord (nerve pathway) has been cut.

How to Minister: (All commands done in Jesus' name.)

1. Command any disease process to go.
2. Command the discs and vertebrae of the back to return to normal position, pressure on the nerves to be released, and the nerves to function normally.

3. Command the electrical and chemical functions of the nervous system to function normally.
4. Command the blood to flow normally throughout the body.
5. Command the electrical and magnetic frequencies to be in harmony and balance.
6. Command all numbness and tingling to go.

OBESITY

Being obese is not the same as being overweight. An adult is considered obese when they weigh 20 percent to 25 percent over their maximum desirable weight. Anyone more than 100 pounds overweight is considered morbidly obese.

Obesity increases the risk for illness and death due to diabetes, stroke, coronary artery disease, hypertension, high cholesterol, and kidney and gallbladder disorders. Obesity is also considered a risk factor for the development of osteoarthritis and sleep apnea. Children of obese parents are ten times more likely to be obese than children with parents of normal weight.

How to Minister: (All commands done in Jesus' name.)

1. Lead them in a prayer of repentance for generational curses.
2. Lead them in a prayer of repentance for lifestyle or diet, if necessary.
3. Command healing of thyroid or other responsible organ.
4. Lay hands on the head and command the "Appestat" (appetite control center) to be readjusted to the normal level and the weight to return to a correct and healthy range.
5. Lead them in a prayer to lay all cares, stress, and worries on the altar of God.
6. Command the metabolism to function normally and the person's weight to be within healthy boundaries.

OBSESSIVE-COMPULSIVE DISORDER (OCD)

A form of mental illness, Obsessive-Compulsive Disorder is an anxiety disorder characterized by obsessions or compulsions. Obsessions are unwanted, inappropriate or senseless intrusive thoughts, ideas, doubts, or impulses that cause intense distress and anxiety. Compulsions are urges to repeat certain behaviors or thoughts in order to decrease anxiety created by obsessions.

Examples of obsessions include exaggerated abnormal overwhelming fears, unwanted or senseless thoughts about harmful, violent, sexually inappropriate, immoral things, or persistent perfection.

Examples of compulsions include excessive hand washing, showering, or cleaning with antibacterial products, excessive rearranging, and continuous repetition of special words to stop unacceptable thoughts.

The exact cause of OCD is unknown, but several factors seem to play a role. Chemical changes in the brain, family history, and genetic inheritance have been linked to OCD. Stressors such as a serious loss, trauma, difficult relationships, job changes, financial problems, or any other stressful situation can trigger or worsen symptoms.

How to Minister: (All commands done in Jesus' name.)

1. Lead them in a prayer of repentance for generational curses.
2. Cast out the spirit of OCD.
3. Lead them in a prayer of repentance and/or forgiveness, if necessary.
4. Command the prions to dissolve and leave the body.
5. Command the electrical and magnetic frequencies to be in harmony and balance.

6. Lead them in a prayer to lay all cares, stress, and worries on the altar of God.
7. Speak peace to them.

OCCUPATIONAL LUNG DISEASE (See Chronic Obstructive Pulmonary disease/COPD.)

OSTEOARTHRITIS (Also called Degenerative Joint Disease, OA, or DJD)

Osteoarthritis causes a gradual deterioration of bone cartilage and the formation of new bone (bone spurs) at various joints throughout the body. Metabolic, genetic, chemical, and mechanical factors play a role in its development. Associated with the aging process, it is the most common form of Arthritis. Almost everyone has some degree of Osteoarthritis by the time they reach seventy years of age.

The cartilage of the affected joint roughens and becomes worn down until bone rubs on bone. Bone spurs usually develop around the joints of the hands, fingers, hips, knees, big toe, and cervical and lumbar spine. Joint damage may begin after trauma to the area, occupational overuse, obesity, or being bow-legged or knock-kneed.

Osteoarthritis discomfort can range from mild to severely debilitating pain with mobility of the joints becoming progressively limited.

How to Minister: (All commands done in Jesus' name.)

1. Lead them in a prayer of repentance for generational curses.
2. Cast out the spirit of Osteoarthritis.
3. Command the cartilage to be restored and the joint to be healed.
4. Lead them in a prayer of forgiveness.

5. Command the electrical and magnetic frequencies to be in harmony and balance.

OSTEOPOROSIS

Osteoporosis, the most common type of bone disease, is the thinning of bone and loss of bone density. Osteoporosis occurs when the body fails to form enough new bone or when old bone is reabsorbed by the body, or both. The leading cause is a drop in estrogen in women at menopause or a drop in testosterone in men. Since calcium and phosphate are essential for normal bone formation, growth and repair, nutritional deficiencies can contribute to development of Osteoporosis in men or women. Other possible causes include hyperthyroidism, excessive use of steroids, being confined to a bed and bone cancers.

Osteopenia (abnormally low bone density) may eventually deteriorate into Osteoporosis if not treated. Dowager's Hump, (a marked abnormal curving of the spine in the area of the shoulder blades/upper back) is due to changes in the bones of the thoracic spine.

The main complication of Osteoporosis or Osteopenia is a fragile bone structure. Fractures occur easily with a simple turn or normal movement and do not heal easily. These fractures can become debilitating.

How to Minister: (All commands done in Jesus' name.)

1. Lead in a prayer of repentance for generational curses.
2. Cast out the spirit of Osteoporosis.
3. Command the body to absorb calcium and other necessary minerals to regenerate new, strong bones in the body.
4. Command the back and sacrum to straighten and all the bones to strengthen.

5. Lead them in a prayer of repentance for forgiveness or to break word curses as needed.
6. Command the pain to go.

OTITIS MEDIA

Otitis Media is an inflammation or infection of the middle ear that occurs when the tube from the back of the throat to the middle ear is blocked. Chronic Otitis Media is diagnosed when the tube becomes blocked repeatedly or remains blocked for long periods due to allergies, multiple infections, ear trauma, or swelling of the adenoids.

An infection may spread into the mastoid bone behind the ear (mastoiditis), or pressure from fluid build-up may rupture the eardrum or damage the bones of the middle ear causing hearing problems.

How to Minister: (All commands done in Jesus' name.)

1. Rebuke the fungus or infection in the ear.
2. Command the tubes to open and fluid to flow normally.
3. Pray for the neck to go into proper alignment.
4. Command the blood to flow into the inner ear and remove impurities.
5. Lead them in a prayer of repentance for generational curses.
2. Command pain to go, and hearing to return to normal.
4. Command the immune system to work properly.

PALSY (See Parkinson's, Cerebral Palsy, Bell's Palsy.)

PANCREATITIS

Pancreatitis is an inflammation or infection of the pancreas, the organ which secretes digestive enzymes and hormones (insulin). Problems in the pancreas can affect function of many other organs of the body and can be very serious.

Causes of Pancreatitis include alcohol abuse, bile duct obstruction, viral infections, traumatic injuries, pancreatic or common bile duct surgical procedures, medications, high lipid levels in the blood, and complications of cystic fibrosis.

How to Minister: (All commands done in Jesus' name.)

1. Curse the root of any viral or bacterial infection.
2. Lead them in a prayer of repentance to break word curses.
3. Command the pain, inflammation, and irritation to go.
4. Command all damaged cells to be healed and normal function returned.

PANIC DISORDER (ALSO CALLED PANIC ATTACK.)

A Panic Disorder involves repeated, unpredictable attacks of intense unreasonable fear accompanied by severe anxiety that may last from minutes to hours.

The exact cause of Panic Disorder is unknown. It is believed that heredity, environment, and previous trauma/experience may influence its development. People with Panic Disorder often undergo medical evaluations for symptoms related to heart attack or other conditions before being diagnosed. There are often extreme changes in behavior.

How to Minister: (All commands done in Jesus' name.)

1. Lead them in a prayer of repentance for generational curses.
2. If possible, find out when it first started and what happened during this time. Minister to the cause.
3. Command the hormones to be in balance and vitamin and mineral absorption to be normal.
4. Lead them in a prayer of repentance, if necessary.
5. Lead them in a prayer to lay all cares, stress, fears, and worries on the altar of God

A person with a Panic Disorder has episodes of intense fear or anxiety that occur suddenly (often without warning), which last from a few minutes to several hours. The typical age of onset is between adolescence and the mid-thirties and can occur in both sexes; however, women are more likely than men to be affected with a Panic Disorder.

The cause for these attacks can vary between people, but they seem to be more common with people who have experienced a serious trauma in their past such as divorce, separation, a troubled family history, abuse, or serious injury.

How to Minister: (All commands done in Jesus' name.)

1. If they are having a Panic Attack, call them by their full Christian name. When you have their attention, say, "Peace, in the name of Jesus."
2. Ask when the Panic Attacks started. Find out what happened to them just before the first occurrence.
3. Lead them in repentance or forgiveness to correct the situation.
4. Command the spirit of fear and or anxiety to leave.
5. Speak peace to them.

PARANOID PERSONALITY DISORDER

Paranoid Personality Disorder is a psychiatric condition characterized by extreme distrust and suspicion of others. These chronic patterns of behavior cause serious problems with work and relationships.

People with Paranoid Personality Disorder are highly suspicious of other people, isolate themselves, have a poor self-image, and exhibit frequent hostility.

How to Minister: (All commands done in Jesus' name.)

1. Lead them in a prayer of repentance for generational curses.

181

2. Cast out the spirit of PPD.
3. Command peace to the brain and to the heart.
4. Command the electrical and magnetic frequencies to be in harmony and balance.
5. Lead them in a prayer to lay all cares, stress, fears, and worries on the altar of God

PARKINSON'S DISEASE

Parkinson's Disease is a disorder of the brain characterized by uncontrollable shaking (tremors) and difficulty with coordination, movement, and walking. The disease causes damage to the part of the brain that controls body movement. It was once called Palsy. Another medical name is Paralysis Agitans.

Parkinson's Disease is caused by progressive deterioration of the nerve cells of the brain that control muscle movement. Parkinsonism may be caused by other disorders or by external factors like certain medications. In addition to the loss of muscle control, some people with Parkinson's Disease become severely depressed. A person with severe Parkinson's may also exhibit overall mental deterioration.

How to Minister: (All commands done in Jesus' name.)

1. Lead them in a prayer of repentance for generational curses.
2. Cast out the spirit of Parkinson's Disease.
3. Command a new brain and nerve tissue that will function normally and produce the correct amount of dopamine.
4. Command healing to all other affected parts of the body.

PERIODONTITIS (Also see Gum Disease.)

Periodontitis is a dental disorder that results from untreated or delayed treatment of gingivitis. This gum disease involves inflammation and infection of the ligaments and bones that support the teeth. When the infection and inflammation spreads from the gums to the ligaments and bone that support the teeth, the teeth loosen and eventually fall out. Periodontitis is the primary cause of tooth loss in adults.

How to Minister: (All commands done in Jesus' name.)

1. Command all infection to go.
2. Command the gums to be healed and tissues restored.
3. Lead them in a prayer or repentance to break word curses.

PHARYNGITIS (See Sore Throat)

PHLEBITIS

Phlebitis is an inflammation of a vein. Thrombophlebitis is vein inflammation related to a blood clot within the vein. Risk factors include prolonged sitting and increased clotting factors in the blood. Specific disorders associated with thrombophlebitis include superficial Phlebitis (affects veins near the skin surface) and Deep Venous Thrombosis (See DVT).

How to Minister: (All commands done in Jesus' name.)

1. Command blood clot to dissolve.
2. Command the infection and inflammation to leave and the blood to function normally.
3. Lead them in a prayer of repentance for generational curses.

PIGEON-TOED

Also called In-toeing, this term describes a person whose feet/toes turn inward. This abnormality can be caused by an inward rotation of the feet, thigh bone, or hip. Babies often appear to be Pigeon-Toed at birth due to their positioning in the womb. It is usually observed in small children who grow out of it by school age.

How to Minister: (All commands done in Jesus' name.)

1. Lead them in a prayer of repentance for generational curses.
2. Command the pelvic bones to rotate outward and into normal position and for the leg bones and foot bones to straighten and go into perfect alignment.

PITUITARY GLAND

The Pituitary Gland is a small gland at the base of the brain. This gland produces hormones that control other glands/organs and influence essential body processes including but not limited to growth of bone structure, sexual maturing, and general metabolism.

Decreased function can cause growth retardation (dwarfism) in childhood and a decrease in other endocrine gland function. Increased function can cause abnormal growth (gigantism) in children and a condition called acromegaly in adults. The pituitary also secretes a hormone to increase uterine contractions and a hormone that increases reabsorption of water by the kidney.

Inflammation, infections, and injury can cause the gland to malfunction, as well as cancer or other tumors. There are many disorders that result from pituitary tumors and disease including but not limited to Cushing's Disease and Addison's Disease.

How to Minister: (All commands done in Jesus' name.)

1. If known, minister to the cause.
2. Lay hands on head and command the pituitary gland to function properly and produce normal amounts of hormones.
3. Command all other affected body parts to be healed and function normally.

PLEURISY

Pleurisy is an inflammation of the tissue lining surrounding the lungs and may develop in the presence of lung inflammation (pneumonia, flu, or tuberculosis), rheumatic diseases, lupus, chest trauma, cancer, pancreatitis, blood clot in the lung, trauma to the chest, or after heart surgery.

The primary symptom is pain over the chest wall during breathing, coughing, and/or chest movement. Fluid often collects at the site of inflammation, which can interfere with breathing.

How to Minister: (All commands done in Jesus' name.)

1. Curse the inflammation and command it to go.
2. Command the fluid to return to normal levels.
3. Command the pain to go and scar tissue to be healed and return to normal tissue.
4. Lead them in a prayer of repentance, if necessary.

PMS (PREMENSTRUAL SYNDROME) (SEE FEMALE PROBLEMS.)

PNEUMONIA

Pneumonia is an inflammation of the lungs caused by an infectious organism such as bacteria, viruses, and fungus. The severity depends on the type of organism causing the Pneumonia as well as age and underlying health condition of the person. Pneumonia is a particular concern for older adults as well as those with chronic illnesses or impaired immune systems.

How to Minister: (All commands done in Jesus' name.)

1. Curse the infection and command the virus or bacteria to die.
2. Command healing and clearing of the lungs of any excess fluid.
3. Command all scarring to be healed.
4. Lead them in a prayer of repentance, if necessary.
5. Command the electrical and magnetic frequencies to be in harmony and balance.

POLIO, POLIOMYELITIS

Poliomyelitis is a communicable disease caused by the polio-virus. This debilitating condition can affect the whole body, including muscles and nerves leading to loss of voluntary movement and muscular wasting. Severe cases may cause permanent paralysis or death.

Transmission of the virus occurs by direct person-to-person contact, by contact with infected secretions, or by contact with infected feces. Even though the last case of Polio was identified in the United States in 1979, Polio is still seen in other parts of the world.

POST-POLIO SYNDROME

Affecting people who have recovered from Polio, Post-Polio Syndrome is a group of disabling symptoms that can appear between 10 and 40 years after the initial illness. Common signs and symptoms include muscle weakness, exhaustion with minimal activity, muscle and joint pain, breathing or swallowing problems, sleep apnea, and poor tolerance of cold temperatures

How to Minister: (All commands done in Jesus' name.)

1. Cast out the spirit of Polio.
2. Command creative miracle to the spinal cord and its damaged nerves, muscles, ligaments, tissues, and tendons to be healed, strengthened, and function normally.

POLYMYOSITIS

Polymyositis is a characterized by inflammation and degeneration of the muscles of the shoulder and hip muscles. The cause of this disorder is unsure. Doctors think that an autoimmune reaction or a viral infection of the skeletal muscle may cause the problem. Polymyositis can be disabling in its more severe forms.

How to Minister: (All commands done in Jesus' name.)

1. Command the immune system to strengthen and function normally.
2. Command new muscles into the body.
3. Command electrical and magnetic frequencies to be in harmony and balance.
4. Lead them in a prayer of forgiveness, if necessary.

POST NASAL DRIP (SEE NOSE.)

POSTPARTUM DEPRESSION (ALSO SEE DEPRESSION.)

Due to the numerous major changes in the life of a new mother, the first few weeks after giving birth can be very challenging for everyone associated with the event. Changes in hormones and weight, and sleep deprivation affect the mother directly; however, relationships with other children, the father of the baby, parents and in-laws, colleagues at work, and friends add to the stress. All of these stress factors contribute to postpartum mood swings and depression. It is commonly called the "baby blues."

How to Minister: (All commands done in Jesus' name.)

1. Command the hormones to come into balance.
2. Command the electrical and magnetic frequencies to be in harmony and balance.
3. Lead them in a prayer or repentance to break word curses.
4. Command the spirit of depression to go.
5. Speak peace to them.

POST-TRAUMATIC STRESS DISORDER (PTSD)

Post-Traumatic Stress Disorder is a mental illness that can develop after a serious physical or emotional traumatic event. It can resolve after a few weeks or last for many years. PTSD can also follow a natural disaster such as flood, fire, hurricane, or events such as war, imprisonment, assault, abuse, or rape.

How to Minister: (All commands done in Jesus' name.)

1. Cast out the spirit of trauma.
2. Minister to the cause through prayers for repentance, forgiveness and to break word curses.
3. Command the hormones to be in balance.
4. Command the electrical and magnetic frequencies to be in harmony and in balance.
5. Speak peace to them.

PREMENSTRUAL SYNDROME (PMS) (See Female Problems.)

PROLAPSED UTERUS (See Female Problems.)

PROSTATE PROBLEMS

The prostate gland produces the fluid that carries sperm during ejaculation. Prostate enlargement is often called Benign Prostatic Hypertrophy or hyperplasia (BPH). It is not cancerous and does not increase the risk for prostate cancer. BPH inhibits the normal function of the testicles, which produce testosterone, the male hormone. As men age, prostate enlargement often causes problems with the normal passage of urine. The exact cause of prostate enlargement is not known.

How to Minister: (All commands done in Jesus' name.)

1. Grow out the legs.
2. Curse the cause of the enlargement.
3. Command the prostate gland to shrink to normal size and to function normally.

4. Command a new prostate when necessary.
5. Command the hormones to be in balance.
6. Command the nerves to work and blood to flow normally.

PSORIASIS

Psoriasis is a common skin irritation and swelling characterized by frequent episodes of redness, itching, and silver scales on the skin. Psoriasis is thought to be an inherited disorder, related to an inflammatory autoimmune response.

Not contagious, Psoriasis may be aggravated by injury or irritation of the skin. It may be more severe in chemically immunosuppressed people or those who have other autoimmune disorders (such as rheumatoid arthritis).

How to Minister: (All commands done in Jesus' name.)

1. Lead them in a prayer of repentance for generational curses.
2. Cast out the spirit of Psoriasis.
3. Rebuke the inflammation, itching, and scaling.
4. Lay hands on the affected areas, commanding healthy new skin cells to replace the affected tissues.

PSYCHOSIS

Psychosis is a serious mental condition. Symptoms include a loss of contact with reality, delusions (false ideas about events or who people are), and hallucinations (seeing or hearing things that aren't there). This condition can be precipitated or influenced by alcohol consumption, certain drugs, bipolar disorders, brain tumors, epilepsy, psychotic depression, schizophrenia, dementia (Alzheimer's and other degenerative brain disorders), Stroke, TIA, or CVA.

How to Minister: (All commands done in Jesus' name.)

1. Cast out the spirit of Psychosis.
2. Lead them in a prayer of repentance for idolatry.

3. Command the chemicals and hormones to be in balance.
4. Command any damaged tissues or organs to be healed and function normally.
5. Speak peace to them.

PULMONARY EDEMA

Pulmonary Edema involves excessive fluid accumulation and swelling within the lungs. Pulmonary Edema is often a complication caused by Congestive Heart Failure. Pulmonary Edema can also be caused by injury from toxins including heat and poisonous gas, severe infection, or an excess of body fluid from kidney failure.

Common symptoms include difficulty breathing, feeling of suffocation, wheezing, gasping for breath, and frothy sputum that may be tinged with blood. Drug-induced Pulmonary Edema is a frequent cause of death in people who abuse narcotics. When not treated, acute Pulmonary Edema can be fatal.

How to Minister: (All commands done in Jesus' name.)

1. Command all excessive fluid to leave the lungs.
2. Command the heart and lungs to be strong and healthy.
3. Command any infections to go and any injured tissues to be restored to normal function.
4. Command new lungs and other organs, if necessary.
5. Command the electrical and magnetic frequencies to be in harmony and balance.

RECTAL PROLAPSE

Rectal Prolapse is the abnormal protrusion of the colon tissue down to or through the rectum. It may appear as a red mass that may be several inches long and may bleed slightly. Rectal Prolapse may occur in children under age 6 and in the elderly. Risk factors for children include health problems such as cystic fibrosis, malnutrition, deformities or physical development problems, straining during bowel movements, and infections. Risk factors for adults include chronic constipation, the effects of surgery or childbirth, and weakness of the lower abdominal muscles.

How to Minister: (All commands done in Jesus' name.)

1. Command the muscles and tendons of the pelvic floor and surrounding structures to strengthen and for the colon to return to its proper position and function.
2. Lead them in a prayer of repentance, if necessary.

RESPIRATORY DISEASE (See Lungs.)

RESTLESS LEG SYNDROME

Restless Leg Syndrome is characterized by uncomfortable sensations in the legs that occurs when a person is relaxed, lying down, or sitting for an extended period of time such as in a car, airplane, or movie theater. The unpleasant sensation is relieved when the legs are moved or stretched by exercise or walking. Symptoms are more noticeable during the night because it usually causes Insomnia and, thus, may also contribute to daytime sleepiness.

Restless Leg Syndrome is associated with Periodic Limb Movement Disorder. The involuntary twitching or kicking leg movements with PLMD while sleeping often results in a poor night's sleep for both the person and their bed partner. Stress generally worsens the syndrome.

How to Minister: (All commands done in Jesus' name.)

1. Lead them in a prayer of repentance for generational curses.
2. Curse the spirit and command it to go.

3. Command the electrical and magnetic frequencies to be in harmony and balance and function normally.
4. Command the nerves and blood circulation to operate normally.
5. Lead them in a prayer to lay all cares, stress, and worries on the altar of God.

RETARDATION

Generally related to significant brain damage or abnormality, Retardation is described as delayed or decreased development of both mental and motor skills. It refers specifically to the delayed development of cognitive skills (such as speech) and delayed development of motor skills (such as walking). Motormental Retardation may be present at birth; however it also can be caused by a disease or injury.

How to Minister: (All commands done in Jesus' name.)

1. Lead them in a prayer of repentance for generational curses.
2. Lay hands on the head, commanding a new brain with normal intelligence.
3. Command the spirit of Retardation to go.

RETINITIS PIGMENTOSA

Retinitis Pigmentosa is an inherited genetic condition of the eye. The progressive degeneration of the retina limits night and peripheral vision. As the disease progresses, blindness may result.

How to Minister: (All commands done in Jesus' name.)

1. Lead them in a prayer of repentance for generational curses.
2. Lay hands on the eyes, commanding a creative miracle to the eye for a new retina and perfect vision.
3. Lead them in a prayer of repentance, if necessary.

RHEUMATIC FEVER

Rheumatic Fever is an inflammatory disease caused by the streptococcus bacteria, the same bacteria that causes strep throat or scarlet fever.

Rheumatic Fever causes problems with joints, skin, and brain as well as damaged heart valves that can lead to further serious heart diseases and/or heart surgery to repair the damage.

How to Minister: (All commands done in Jesus' name.)

1. Rebuke the infectious process.
2. Command the joints, heart, and other tissues of the body to be healed and function normally.
3. Command any damaged organs to be healed and function properly.
4. Lead them in a prayer of repentance, if necessary.

RHEUMATOID ARTHRITIS (Also called RA.)

Rheumatoid Arthritis is a chronic inflammatory disease that affects the joints of the body and surrounding tissues as well as other organ systems. Considered an autoimmune disease, it is felt that infectious, genetic, and hormonal factors may contribute to RA development.

Rheumatoid Arthritis usually begins gradually as joint pain with accompanying warmth, swelling, tenderness, and stiffness of the joint after inactivity. Whereas Osteoarthritis can be isolated to one side of the body, RA usually affects joints on both sides of the body equally.

The wrists, fingers, knees, feet, and ankles are the sites most commonly affected. Hands with RA have characteristic enlarged deformed joints. Joint destruction and deformities can become seriously debilitating as the disease progresses.

How to Minister: (All commands done in Jesus' name.)

1. Cast out the spirit of Rheumatoid Arthritis.
2. Command all inflammation and swelling to be healed and pain to go.
3. Command the cartilage to be restored to normal and all deformities to disappear.
4. Lead them in the prayer of forgiveness.
5. Command the immune system to function properly.

RHINITIS (See Allergies, Influenza and Nose.)

RINGING IN THE EARS (See Tinnitus.)

ROTATOR CUFF

Vital to the function of the shoulder, the Rotator Cuff is a group of muscles and tendons that control the rotation of the shoulder and hold the arm in its "ball and socket" joint. The tendons hold the powerful shoulder muscles to the shoulder and arm bones while allowing the arm muscles to reach outwards and upwards.

The tendons can be damaged from overuse or injury. The most common symptoms of a rotator cuff tear may include: recurrent pain, shoulder pain that prevents sleeping on the injured side, limited mobility of the arm, and muscle weakness. A complete separation (or tear) to the Rotator Cuff usually requires surgical repair.

How to Minister: (All commands done in Jesus' name.)

1. Command the muscles, tendons, and ligaments to strengthen and go back to their normal length and strength.
2. Command the Rotator Cuff to be healed and all infection and inflammation to leave.

3. Command the socket to be well lubricated and the cartilage to be restored.
4. Cast out the spirit of Arthritis, if necessary.
5. Grow out the arms.
6. Command the pain to go and command full mobility to be restored.

SALIVARY GLANDS

The Salivary Glands produce saliva, which moistens food to aid chewing and swallowing. Saliva contains enzymes that begin the digestive process, cleans the mouth by washing away bacteria and food particles, keeps the mucous membranes of the mouth moist, and helps to keep dentures or orthodontic appliances in place.

Salivary glands are located in each cheek in front of the ears, at the back of the mouth on both sides of the jaw and under the floor of the mouth. All of these glands empty saliva into the mouth at various locations within the mouth. The Salivary Glands may become inflamed (irritated) because of infection, tumors, or stones. Mumps is an inflammation of the salivary glands located in front of the ears.

How to Minister: (All commands done in Jesus' name.)

1. Command any infection, tumor, or stones to leave.
2. Command new salivary glands.
3. Lead them in a prayer of repentance to break word curses.

SCARS, KELOIDS, ADHESIONS

A Scar is a mark left on the skin after a wound, burn, or sore has healed. A Scar often fades over time.

Keloids are an abnormal overgrowth of scar tissue at the site of the injury such as surgical incisions, traumatic wounds, vaccination sites, burns, chickenpox, acne, or even minor scratches. After several years, most Keloids will flatten and become less noticeable; however, they may become irritated from rubbing or friction. Extensive Keloids may severely limit movement and can be very debilitating. They may cause cosmetic changes and affect the appearance.

Usually following surgery, inflammation, or an injury, Adhesions are an abnormal joining of normally unconnected body parts or organs inside the body. The affected tissues bond to other tissue or organs, much like the process of forming scar tissue.

Adhesions of the iris to the lens of the eye can lead to glaucoma. In the intestines, Adhesions can cause partial or complete bowel obstruction necessitating emergency life-saving surgery. Lower abdominal Adhesions can cause infertility and reproductive problems.

How to Minister: (All commands done in Jesus' name.)

1. Command the scar tissue to be dissolved.
2. Command all organs and structures to be healed and to function normally.

SCHIZOPHRENIA

Schizophrenia is a serious mental disorder with symptoms of unstable emotions, withdrawal, delusions, hallucinations, abnormal behavior, disordered thinking, catatonic behavior (curled up in fetal position), or flat effect.

How to Minister: (All commands done in Jesus' name.)

1. Lead them in a prayer of repentance for generational curses.
2. Command all the chemicals and hormones in the body to be in balance.

3. Command the brain to process information properly.
4. Command a new brain.
5. Lead them in a prayer of repentance, if necessary.

SCIATICA

Sciatica is a condition involving pain, weakness, numbness, or tingling in the leg. It is usually caused by injury or compression of the sciatic nerve located in the back of the leg. This nerve controls the muscles on the back of the knee and lower leg and provides sensation to the back of the thigh, part of the lower leg, and the sole of the foot.

Problems can develop from fractures of the pelvis, trauma to the buttocks or thigh, prolonged sitting or lying with pressure on the buttocks, diabetes, tumor, abscess, or by bleeding in the pelvis. Note: A ruptured lumbar disc in the spine may cause symptoms very similar to the symptoms of sciatic nerve dysfunction.

How to Minister: (All commands done in Jesus' name.)

1. Grow out the legs.
2. Command the lumbar vertebra and sacrum to return to normal alignment and the supporting muscles to strengthen.
3. Command all the discs to go back into place and relieve all pressure on the nerves.
4. Command the spirit of Sciatica to go and the nerve to be released.
5. Lead them in a prayer of repentance, if necessary.

SCLERODERMA (ALSO CALLED SYSTEMIC SCLEROSIS.)

Scleroderma is a debilitating autoimmune disease in which the skin becomes progressively hard and thickened. Scleroderma can also cause these changes in blood vessels, skeletal muscles, and internal organs causing many other complications that can be fatal.

How to Minister: (All commands done in Jesus' name.)

1. Cast out the spirit of Scleroderma.
2. Command the immune system to be healed and return to normal function.
3. Command new tissue to replace the damaged areas of the skin and all affected internal organs.
4. Command the electrical and magnetic frequencies to come into harmony and balance.

SCOLIOSIS

Scoliosis is an abnormal curvature of the spine. Causes of scoliosis include congenital deformities and neuromuscular diseases such as cerebral palsy, muscular dystrophy, spinal deformities, and polio.

Scoliosis may be suspected when one shoulder appears to be higher than the other or the pelvis appears to be tilted.

How to Minister: (All commands done in Jesus' name.)

1. Lead them in a prayer of repentance for generational curses.
2. Cast out the spirit of Scoliosis.
3. Command the bones in the back, the ribs, and supportive structures of the body to come into normal and perfect alignment.
4. Command the muscles, tendons, and ligaments to strengthen.
5. Grow out the legs.
6. Grow out the arms.
7. Do the pelvic adjustment.

SEIZURES (ALSO SEE EPILEPSY.)

A Seizure is a sudden, excessive, abnormal electrical activity within the brain. Abnormally synchronized electrical messages sent from brain cells to muscles causes a seizure or convulsion, a violent shaking of the body or limbs caused by uncontrollable muscle contractions.

Symptoms include loss of consciousness with twitching or shaking of the body; however, some seizures consist only of blank stares for a few moments. Occasionally, Seizures can cause temporary abnormal sensations or visual disturbances.

Known causes of Seizures include: metabolic disturbances (such as a malfunction of the kidney or liver; insulin shock with Diabetes), brain injury, interrupted blood circulation (such as an aneurysm or stroke), toxic substances (drugs, alcohol), infection (such as meningitis or encephalitis), birth defects, or brain tumor.

A typical Grand Mal Seizure causes a loss of consciousness and falling down, loss of bowel or bladder control, and rhythmic convulsions. Most Grand Mal Seizures last from thirty seconds to five minutes and may have residual headache, drowsiness, or confusion.

Focal Seizures involve only a few muscles, such as one side of the face or one arm or leg. Epilepsy is a chronic disorder with recurrent episodes called Petit Mal Seizures.

How to Minister: (All commands done in Jesus' name.)

1. Lead them in a prayer of repentance for generational curses.
2. Curse the spirit and command it to go.
3. Command the electrical and magnetic frequencies to be in harmony and balance and function normally.
4. Command a new brain.

SHORT LEG

Unless there is a birth defect or bone loss, short legs are caused by a lower back problem that draws up the ligaments, muscles, and bones, making the leg appear to be "short."

How to Minister: (All commands done in Jesus' name.)

1. Grow out the legs.
2. Command the back to be healed and muscles, tendons, and ligaments to be their normal length and strength and to go into proper alignment.
3. If the leg is actually shorter or smaller, command a creative miracle. Command the leg to grow to normal length and size.

SICKLE-CELL ANEMIA

An abnormal type of hemoglobin within the red blood cells causes Sickle-Cell Anemia, an inherited disease. The red blood cells are misshapen, die earlier than usual, and may block small vessels with blood clots. Healthy red blood cells and hemoglobin are necessary to carry oxygen to the body. When oxygen cannot reach the body cells, tissue damage occurs causing a very painful "sickle cell crisis." When the damaged tissues are located in a vital organ, serious complications can develop

How to Minister: (All commands done in Jesus' name.)

1. Lead in a prayer of repentance for generational curses.
2. Cast out the spirit of Sickle-Cell Anemia.
3. Command the defective genes to be restored to normal.
4. Command the marrow to produce normal blood cells and the affected organs and tissues of the body to be healed.

SINUS PROBLEMS

Sinusitis refers to inflammation or infection of the sinus cavities. Allergic reactions to environmental pollutants such as smoke, smog, or pollen can contribute to the irritation and inflammation. Sinus cavities, located around the forehead, cheeks, and eyes, are lined with mucous membranes. When the membranes become inflamed, the sinuses can be blocked with mucus and can easily become infected. Generally caused by a viral, bacterial, or fungal infection, Sinusitis often occurs in conjunction with respiratory infections such as colds or rhinitis.

How to Minister: (All commands done in Jesus' name.)

1. Rebuke the infection and curse any allergies.
2. Lay hands on the face and command the sinuses to drain, open up, and be healed.
3. Grow out the arms.
4. Command the blood vessels to open and reduce swelling and inflammation of the areas.
5. Lead them in a prayer of repentance, if necessary.

SJOGREN'S SYNDROME

Sjogren's (SHOW-grins) Syndrome is an autoimmune disease often defined by its two most common symptoms which are dry eyes and a dry mouth. It often accompanies other autoimmune disorders such as rheumatoid arthritis or lupus.

In Sjogren's Syndrome, the mucous membranes and glands of the eyes and mouth malfunction causing decreased production of tears and saliva. This can lead to problems with swallowing, increased dental cavities, light-sensitive eyes, corneal ulcers, and damage to tissues of the lungs, kidneys, and liver.

How to Minister: (All commands done in Jesus' name.)

1. Rebuke the abnormal disease process.
2. Command the all affected tissues of the body to be healed and function normally.

3. Command the immune system and any damaged organs to be healed and function properly.
4. Lead them in a prayer of repentance, if necessary.

SLEEP DISORDERS (Also see Insomnia, Snoring, and Restless Leg Syndrome.)

Sleep Disorders involve any difficulties related to sleep including difficulty falling or staying asleep, inability to stay awake, excessive time spent asleep, or abnormal behaviors associated with sleep.

Insomnia or Problems Falling and Staying Asleep

Insomnia includes difficulty falling asleep and staying asleep, intermittent wakefulness, and awakening too early in the morning.

Some common factors associated with nighttime insomnia include: physical illness, anxiety, increased stress, caffeine, alcohol, drugs, smoking, excessive noise or light, pain, or too much daytime napping.

Insomnia can lead to daytime drowsiness, poor concentration, and the inability to feel rested in the morning. Everyone has an occasional sleepless night; however, Insomnia can impair a person's ability to adequately complete daily responsibilities because of excess tiredness or trouble with concentration.

How to Minister: (All commands done in Jesus' name.)

1. Lead them in a prayer of repentance, if necessary.
2. Command the sleep center of the brain to operate normally.
3. Lead them in a prayer to lay all cares, stress, and worries on the altar of God.
4. Repent for not taking a Sabbath's days rest, if necessary.

NARCOLEPSY

Narcolepsy is a chronic neurological sleep disorder characterized by overwhelming uncontrollable daytime drowsiness and sudden sleep attacks. People with Narcolepsy fall asleep inappropriately without warning, anywhere, and at any time regardless of the circumstances. They also exhibit other symptoms that may include sleep paralysis and hallucinations.

Narcolepsy can cause serious problems in both professional and personal lives. Sleep attacks may result in physical harm if they occur during everyday activities such as driving a car, using dangerous equipment, lighting a fire, or cutting food.

SLEEP APNEA

Sleep Apnea is a condition that most commonly affects obese people, but it may affect anyone with a short neck or a small jaw, regardless of their actual weight. The disorder causes breathing to stop intermittently during normal sleep, waking the person repeatedly. Loud snoring and labored breathing are frequent symptoms that the airway is blocked. People with Sleep Apnea have difficulty achieving prolonged, deep restorative sleep. This results in excessive daytime sleepiness, also a symptom of Narcolepsy.

Because Sleep Apnea causes sudden drops in blood oxygen levels, people with Sleep Apnea are at higher risk for complications such as brain damage, stroke, high blood pressure, or sudden death. Children with Sleep Apnea may be hyperactive and may be diagnosed with ADHD. Overgrown tonsils and/or adenoids are considered the most common cause of childhood Sleep Apnea.

SLEEPWALKING

Sleepwalking usually occurs a few hours after a person has fallen asleep. Sleepwalkers do not only walk. They may do such things as change their clothes, move furniture, or just sit up in bed. Afterwards, they cannot remember any of their actions. Episodes may be related to extreme fatigue or anxiety.

How to Minister: (All commands done in Jesus' name.)

1. Lead them in a prayer of repentance for generational curses.
2. Lead them in a prayer to lay all cares, stress, fears, and worries on the altar of God.
3. Command all hormones to be in balance.
4. Command the electrical and magnetic frequencies to be in harmony and balance.
5. Command the neck to come into alignment and for all obstructions in the breathing pathways to be removed.
6. Command the muscles in the upper part of the throat to function normally during sleep.
7. Command any ungodly spirit to come out.
8. Speak a blessing of restful and restorative peaceful sleep.
9. Command the sleep center of the brain to operate normally.

SNORING

Snoring is loud, hoarse, or harsh breathing sounds that happen while a person is asleep. It is often disruptive to the person as well as to others within hearing distance. While taking a breath, air flows past the relaxed tissues in the throat causing the tissues to vibrate, creating hoarse or harsh sounds.

Snoring may possibly be an indication of an underlying disorder such as chronic nasal congestion, deviated nasal septum, sleep apnea, or enlarged tonsils or adenoids. Other contributing factors include being overweight; the relaxing effects of sleeping pills, antihistamines, or alcohol at bedtime; or sleeping on the back allowing the tongue to relax back into the throat.

How to Minister: (All commands done in Jesus' name.)

1. Lead them in a prayer of repentance for generational curses.
2. Command the muscles and tissues of the upper throat to function normally during sleep.
3. Command any blockages in air pathways to be removed.

SORE THROAT (ALSO SEE INFLUENZA, COLD, LARYNGITIS.)

A Sore Throat causes discomfort, pain, or scratchiness in the throat and often makes swallowing painful. A Sore Throat usually occurs in combination with other signs and symptoms of an upper respiratory infection, but can occur by itself. Like a common Cold, the majority of Sore Throats are caused by a viral infection.

Mononucleosis is a much longer-lived viral illness that causes a very painful Sore Throat and problems swallowing. Other viral illnesses that include a Sore Throat include measles, chickenpox, and Croup.

Bacterial infections associated with a Sore Throat can include strep throat, tonsillitis, and diphtheria. Other common causes of Sore Throat include allergic reactions, excessively dry indoor air, chronic nasal congestion causing constant mouth breathing, environmental air pollution, inhaling smoke, alcohol, spicy foods, muscle strain of the throat, acid reflux (GERDS), or vomiting.

How to Minister: (All commands done in Jesus' name.)

1. Curse the root of any viral or bacterial infection.
2. Lead them in a prayer of repentance for word curses.
3. Command the pain, inflammation, or irritation to go.
4. Command any allergic reaction to disappear.
5. Command the electrical and magnetic frequencies to be in harmony and balance.

SPASTICITY

Spasticity is marked by stiff or rigid muscles and exaggerated reflexes which interferes with walking, movement, or speech.

Spasticity can be seen with any form of brain, spine, or nerve damage including Multiple Sclerosis or Cerebral Palsy. Symptoms include exaggerated knee-jerk reflexes, repetitive uncontrollable jerky limb movements, unusual posturing, and carrying the shoulder, arm, wrist, and fingers at an abnormal angle. Spasticity may also interfere with speech patterns. Severe, long-term Spasticity may lead to contractured muscles causing joints to be bent in a fixed position.

How to Minister: (All commands done in Jesus' name.)

1. Command the nervous system to be healed, completely restored, and function normally.
2. Speak a new brain, if necessary.
3. Command the hormones to be in balance.
4. Command the electrical and magnetic frequencies to be in harmony and balance.
5. Cast out the spirit of trauma.
6. Lead them in a prayer of forgiveness, if necessary.

SPINA BIFIDA

Spina Bifida is a serious congenital birth defect. The backbone and spinal canal do not close properly before birth leaving the spinal cord and its protective covering membranes protruding from the infant's back.

The terms Myelomeningocele or Open Spina Bifida may be used. The baby is prone to life-threatening infections such as meningitis and other neurological problems such as paralysis, loss of bowel and bladder control, seizures, and learning disabilities as well as other medical complications.

How to Minister: (All commands done in Jesus' name.)

1. Lead them in a prayer of repentance for generational curses.
2. Command the spine to close completely.
3. Command a new spine, if necessary.
4. Command any scarring from surgery to dissolve.
5. Command the brain and all nerve tissue and pathways to be totally healed and function normally.

SPRAIN (OR STRAIN)

During physical activity, sudden pain and swelling around a joint or a muscle may occur when injured. The injury may be a Sprain or a Strain.

Sprains occur when a ligament is stretched too far or torn. Ligaments are bands of tough fibrous tissue that connect one bone to another and stabilize the joints. The common locations for a Sprain include the ankles, wrists, or knees. A Strain is a stretching or tearing of muscle tissue. People sometimes called this a "pulled muscle." Hamstring and back injuries are examples of common Strains.

Since symptoms of a Strain, Sprain or fracture may be similar, an X-ray is often necessary to determine the extent and specific type of injury.

How to Minister: (All commands done in Jesus' name.)

1. Command the tendons, muscles, and ligaments to be restored and strengthened.
2. Grow out the arms or the legs.
3. Command the pain and all inflammation to go.

STOMACH PROBLEM

This includes any problem associated with the stomach.

How to Minister: (All commands done in Jesus' name.)

1. If possible, determine specific problem and command it to be healed or new part created and to function normally.
2. Lead them in a prayer to lay cares, stress, and worries on the altar of God.
3. Lead them in a prayer for repentance to break word curses.

STREP THROAT (See Sore Throat.)

STRESS (Also see Post Traumatic Stress Disorder.)

Stress can come from any situation that causes frustration, anger, or anxiety. Stress is a normal part of life. In small quantities, stress can motivate a person to be more productive. However, too much stress can be harmful. It can exacerbate illnesses like infection, heart disease, or depression.

Persistent Stress can also precipitate unhealthy behaviors like overeating, alcohol, or drugs. Emotional problems such as grief or depression or health conditions such as an overactive thyroid, low blood sugar, or heart attack can also cause Stress. People, money problems, work problems, disasters, injuries—stress comes from numerous directions.

How to Minister: (All commands done in Jesus' name.)

1. Lead them in a prayer to lay all cares, stress, fears, and worries on the altar of God.
2. Command all chemicals and hormones to return to normal.
3. Lead them in a prayer of repentance, if necessary.
4. Speak peace to them.

STROKE (CVA—Cardiovascular Accident)

A stroke is an interruption of the blood supply to any part of the brain depriving the brain tissue of the oxygen and nutrients necessary to function properly. If the flow of blood to the brain is interrupted for longer than a few minutes, brain cells die causing permanent damage. The area of the brain that is affected can no longer communicate to the body and loss of function results. An interruption can be caused by either blood clots, bleeding into the brain (aneurysm or blood vessel burst from uncontrolled high blood pressure), or particles that block the blood flow (Atherosclerosis). A leading cause of death in the USA, it is also a leading cause of adult disability.

Symptoms of a Stroke and the after effects are often the same: numbness, weakness, or paralysis on one side of the body, loss of speech, problems with vision, dizziness, loss of coordination, confusion, and loss of memory. If severe, the Stroke can leave the person totally disabled and dependent on another person for all cares and movements.

A "mild stroke" or TIA is a temporary interruption of the blood flow to a part of the brain. (Official term is Transient Ischemic Attack). Initially, the symptoms may be the same as a Stroke; however, the symptoms last from a few minutes to a few days. A TIA usually disappears without leaving apparent permanent effects; however, it is considered a warning that a Stroke could follow.

How to Minister: (All commands done in Jesus' name.)

1. Cast out the spirit of death.
2. Command any blockage to dissolve and be removed.
3. Command all damaged tissue of the brain and other affected body parts be healed, restored, and function normally.
4. Command a new brain, if necessary.
5. Command the communication from the brain to the body to be restored and function normally.

STUTTERING

Stuttering means hesitation, repetition, or stumbling over words while speaking. Young children may stutter but they usually grow out of it as their confidence increases. For some, the stuttering progresses from repetition of consonants to repetition of words and phrases. Stuttering may have genetic implications or it may be associated with some neurological deficits.

Surprisingly, people with significant speech difficulty often do not stutter when singing or are alone talking to themselves.

How to Minister: (All commands done in Jesus' name.)

1. Lead them in a prayer of repentance for generational curses.
2. Command the nervous system to operate properly.
3. Command the spirit of trauma to leave.

SUICIDE

Suicide is the act of intentionally taking one's own life. Suicidal behavior includes any deliberate life-threatening act such as taking a drug overdose or deliberately crashing a car. Suicidal behaviors are often associated with emotional disturbances such as depression, bipolar disorder, or schizophrenia.

Suicidal behaviors can often appear in response to overwhelming situations such as the death of a loved one, emotional trauma, serious physical illness, unemployment, money problems, and alcohol or drug dependence.

Suicide attempts must be considered very serious and professional help should be found immediately. Those with suicidal thoughts or tendencies often believe that they are doing their friends and relatives a favor by removing themselves from the world.

How to Minister: (All commands done in Jesus' name.)

1. Lead them in a prayer of repentance.
2. Command all chemicals and hormones to be in balance.

Prayers for Various Conditions

3. Lead them in a prayer of forgiveness and repentance to break word curses.
4. Cast out the spirit of Suicide.
5. Lead them in a prayer to lay all cares, stress, and worries on the altar of God.
6. Ask them to repeat the declaration "I choose life!" many times.

SWELLING (See Edema.)

TAILBONE (Coccyx)

Tailbone trauma is an injury to the lower tip of the spine. Trauma usually involves bruising of the bone or pulling of the adjacent ligaments. Falling backward onto a hard surface, such as a slippery floor or ice, is the most common cause of this injury. These injuries are painful and make sitting very uncomfortable if not impossible.

How to Minister: (All commands done in Jesus' name.)
1. Command the tailbone to go back into place.
2. Command any fractures, bruising, or swelling to be healed.
3. Command all pain to go.

TEETH (Also See Periodontitis, Gingivitis, and Gum Disease.)

Widely spaced or crooked teeth can be a temporary condition related to normal growth and development before adult teeth develop in the mouth. Wide spacing can also result from abnormal growth of the maxilla or jawbone.

Teeth—Overbite or Underbite

An Overbite or Underbite indicates abnormal alignment of the teeth. Overbite means the upper front teeth protrude too far

211

over the lower teeth when the mouth is closed. An Underbite means the lower teeth protrude outward further than the upper teeth. A small child sucking their thumb can cause either of these abnormalities. These conditions can also be caused by the jaw itself being displaced by an injury.

How to Minister: (All commands done in Jesus' name.)

1. Lead them in a prayer of repentance for generational curses.
2. Lay hands on the jaw and command the jaw to be adjusted to allow enough space for the teeth to be in proper alignment.
3. Command the teeth to line up properly.

TEETH—GRINDING (ALSO SEE TMJ.)

Teeth grinding usually occurs at night during sleep. Some people unconsciously clench their teeth together during waking hours when they feel anxious or tense; however most grind their teeth during sleep. Persistent grinding can lead to jaw disorders (TMJ), headaches, damaged teeth and other problems.

Psychological factors may include anxiety, stress, tension, anger, frustration, aggression, and competitive or hyperactive personality type. In some children, it may be related to growth and development. It can be common in those with cerebral palsy or severe mental retardation; however, it can be a complication of other disorders such as Huntington's disease or Parkinson's disease.

How to Minister: (All commands done in Jesus' name.)

1. Grow out the arms.
2. Command the affected nerves to be released.
3. Lead them in a prayer of forgiveness, if necessary.
4. Lead them in a prayer to lay all cares, stress, fears, and worries on the altar of God.

212

TOOTHACHE/TOOTH DECAY

A Toothache is pain in or around a tooth. It is generally the result of Tooth Decay or an infection of the area. Tooth Decay may be caused by poor dental hygiene, although the tendency to get Tooth Decay is partly inherited.

How to Minister: (All commands done in Jesus' name.)

1. Curse the decay and command the pain to go.
2. Lay hands on the affected area and command the teeth to be restored.
3. Command new teeth.

TENDONITIS

Tendonitis is inflammation, irritation, and swelling of a tendon, the fibrous connecting band of tissue that joins muscle to bone. Tendonitis can occur from an injury, overuse, or with aging as the tendon loses elasticity. It can also appear with diseases such as rheumatoid arthritis or diabetes. Tendonitis can affect any tendon of the body, but some common sites include the shoulder, the wrist, the heel (Achilles tendonitis), and the elbow (called "Tennis Elbow").

Caused by repetitively twisting the wrist or forearm, Tennis Elbow is an inflammation, soreness, or pain on the outside of the upper arm near the elbow. The injury is often associated with tennis players; thus the condition has became known as "Tennis Elbow," but any activity that involves repetitive twisting of the wrist (like using a screwdriver) can lead to this condition.

How to Minister: (All commands done in Jesus' name.)

1. Command all inflammation, pain, swelling, and irritation to go.
2. Grow out the arms or legs of the affected area.

3. Command the muscles, tendons, ligaments, and surrounding tissues to be healed, go back to their proper length and strength, and function normally.
4. If worn out from use, command new tendons and ligaments.
5. Lead them in a prayer of repentance if necessary.

THYROID DISEASE (ALSO SEE GOITER.)

The thyroid gland is located in the base of the neck near the voice box and windpipe. The gland produces a thyroid hormone necessary to regulate the metabolism of the body.

Thyroid diseases include hyperthyroidism (produces too much hormone), hypothyroidism (produces too little of the hormone), benign (noncancerous) thyroid disease, or thyroid cancer.

How to Minister: (All commands done in Jesus' name.)
1. Lead them in a prayer of repentance for generational curses.
2. Command a new thyroid that works properly.
3. Command any swelling to leave.
4. Command all hormones to be in balance.
5. Curse the root of cancer, if necessary.

TIC DOULOUREUX (ALSO KNOWN AS PAINFUL TWITCH.)

Trigeminal Neuralgia (Tic Douloureux) is a very painful disorder of the "trigeminal" nerve located in the face. The nerve controls sensation of the face, tears, and saliva production. The sudden, uncontrolled sharp pain often causes the person to wince or twitch. It may be caused by a tumor on or near the trigeminal nerve or pressure on the nerve root by a blood vessel.

How to Minister: (All commands done in Jesus' name.)
1. Lead them in a prayer of repentance for generational curses.

2. Command all the pressure on the nerves to be healed and all nerves to function normally.
3. Curse the disease and command the spirit to go.
4. Lead them in a prayer of repentance or forgiveness, if necessary.

TINNITUS

Tinnitus is the medical term for hearing abnormal noises in the ears with no obvious source of the sounds. The noises may be soft, loud, ringing, blowing, roaring, buzzing, hissing, humming, whistling, or sizzling. Tinnitus is common and may last only a few minutes. However, constant or frequent Tinnitus is stressful and can interfere with concentration or sleep.

Tinnitus can be a symptom of an ear problem, including infection, excess wax in the ear, or injury from loud noises. Alcohol, caffeine, antibiotics, aspirin, or other drugs can also cause ear noise. Occasionally, it is a symptom of high blood pressure, an allergy, or anemia.

How to Minister: (All commands done in Jesus' name.)

1. Lead them in a prayer of repentance for generational curses.
2. Curse the root cause and command it to go.
3. Command the blood to flow through the ear canal properly.

TEMPOROMANDIBULAR JOINTS (TMJ)

The Temporomandibular Joints connect your lower jaw to your skull on each side of your head just in front of your ears. Symptoms of problems include popping sounds in the jaw, the inability to fully open the mouth, jaw pain, headaches, earaches, toothaches, and various other types of facial pain.

Many TMJ symptoms are caused by the effects of physical stress or abnormalities around the joint including the muscles of the jaw, face, and neck; the teeth; the cartilage disc at the joint; and nearby ligaments, blood vessels, and nerves.

Clenching and grinding the teeth during the day and at night causes pressure on the muscles, tissues, and other structures around your jaw and will exacerbate the TMJ condition/symptoms.

How to Minister: (All commands done in Jesus' name.)

1. Lead them in a prayer of repentance for generational curses.
2. Command the jaw to go back into place and pain to go.
3. Command the tissues, ligaments, and cartilage to be healed and adjusted to the right alignment.
4. Lead them in a prayer of repentance to break word curses.

THROMBOPHLEBITIS (See Phlebitis and DVT.)

TONSILLITIS

Tonsillitis is inflammation of the tonsils or lymph nodes in the back of the mouth and top of the throat that normally filter out bacteria and prevent infection in the body. If the tonsils become overwhelmed by bacteria or viral infection, inflammation, swelling, painful swallowing, and a very sore throat develop.

How to Minister: (All commands done in Jesus' name.)

1. Rebuke the infection and command it to be gone.
2. Command the tonsils to return to normal size and to function normally.
3. Command all pain to go.

TOOTHACHE/TOOTH DECAY (See Teeth.)

TOURETTE SYNDROME

Gilles de la Tourette Syndrome, also called simply Tourette Syndrome, is a disorder characterized by tics that are repeated, sudden, rapid, involuntary body movements. Tics can include eye blinking, repeated throat clearing, sniffing, arm thrusting, kicking, shoulder shrugging, or jumping.

It may be an inherited disorder transmitted through one or more genes. The most common initial symptom is a facial tic with other tics to follow. Contrary to popular belief, use of inappropriate words occurs rarely.

How to Minister: (All commands done in Jesus' name.)

1. Lead them in a prayer of repentance for generational curses.
2. Command the spirit of Tourette Syndrome to go.
3. Command the electrical and magnetic frequencies to be in harmony and balance.
4. Lead them in a prayer of repentance, if necessary.

TRAUMATIC EVENT (See also PTSD—Post Traumatic Stress Disorder.)

A Traumatic Event is any threatening experience or event that causes physical, emotional, psychological distress or harm. It is perceived and experienced as a threat to one's safety or to the stability of one's environment.

How to Minister: (All commands done in Jesus' name.)

1. Command the spirit of trauma and fear to go.
2. Lead them in a prayer to lay all cares, stress, fears, and worries on the altar of God.
3. Lead them in a prayer of forgiveness or repentance.
4. Speak peace to them.

TREMOR, ESSENTIAL

Essential Tremor is a nerve disorder that causes uncontrollable shaking of the hands, head, or voice when a person is attempting to perform a task.

The most common form of abnormal tremors, it occurs when one part of the brain does not function normally. Stress, fatigue, anger, fear, caffeine, and cigarettes may temporarily worsen the condition.

How to Minister: (All commands done in Jesus' name.)
1. Command the brain to function properly.
2. Command the electrical and magnetic frequencies to be in harmony and balance.
3. Command the hormones to be in balance.
4. Lead them in a prayer of repentance when necessary.
5. Lead them in a prayer to lay all cares, stress, fears, and worries on the altar of God.

TRIGEMINAL NEURALGIA (See Tic Douloureux.)

TUMOR (Also see Cancer.)

A Tumor is an abnormal growth of tissue found anywhere in the body. Tumors are classified as either benign (slow-growing and harmless) or malignant (fast growing, can spread throughout the body and can become life-threatening). Malignant Tumors are called Cancers.

The immune system does not or cannot recognize the precipitating factors that can include tobacco usage, obesity, sedentary lifestyle, excessive alcohol consumption, radiation, genetic abnormalities, excessive sunlight exposure, benzene, and a number of other chemicals and toxins.

How to Minister: (All commands done in Jesus' name.)
1. Curse the root of the Tumor and command it to dissolve.
2. Lead in repentance for bitterness or unforgiveness, if necessary.

3. Command electrical and magnetic frequencies to come into harmony and balance.
4. Curse any prions and command them to be discarded.
5. Command the immune system to operate properly.
6. Lead them in a prayer of repentance for lifestyle or diet, if necessary.

ULCER

An Ulcer is an open sore on a body surface. It can develop on the skin or mucous membranes either inside or outside of the body. They may be caused by inflammation, infection (stomach ulcer), or malignant conditions (tumors); excessive stress, poor diet, sedentary lifestyle (decubitus or pressure sores); medication side effects (peptic ulcer), drug or alcohol abuse (esophageal ulcers); smoking, stress; or pressure (bed sores). Many other diseases exacerbate Ulcer formation and make healing difficult such as Crohn's Disease, Herpes, Diabetes, or circulation problems (Peripheral Vascular Disease).

How to Minister: (All commands done in Jesus' name.)

1. Command all tissues in the affected area to be healed.
2. Command all underlying disease processes to cease and all body systems to function normally.
3. Lead them in a prayer to lay all cares, stress, and worries on the altar of God.
4. Lead them in a prayer of repentance for diet or lifestyle, if necessary.

URINARY TRACT INFECTION (UTI)

A Urinary Tract Infection, or UTI, is an infection that can develop anywhere within the urinary tract including the kidneys, the ureters (the tubes that take urine from each kidney to the bladder), the bladder, or the urethra (the tube that drains urine from the bladder to the outside).

Most Urinary Tract Infections are caused by bacteria entering the area from outside the body. The most common cause is the bacteria called E Coli that comes from feces (stool). Elderly people (especially those who have chronic incontinence) and people with diabetes are more prone to infections. Cystitis is the term to describe an inflammation of the urinary bladder. Nephritis is an inflammation of the kidneys. Proper cleansing after toileting can often prevent UTIs.

How to Minister: (All commands done in Jesus' name.)

1. Rebuke the infection and command it to go.
2. Command the kidneys, bladder, and all the tissues and nerves to be restored to normal structure and function.
3. Lead them in a prayer of repentance, if necessary.

VARICOSE VEINS

Varicose Veins are large, twisted, and painful superficial veins. Normally, valves within the veins keep blood moving toward the heart. With varicose veins, the valves do not function properly, blood flow slows down, and the abnormal pooling of blood causes the vein to enlarge.

The most frequently identified causes include congenitally defective valves, thrombophlebitis, and pregnancy. Prolonged standing and increased pressure within the abdomen (obesity or tumors) may increase the development of varicose veins or aggravate the condition.

How to Minister: (All commands done in Jesus' name.)

1. Lead them in a prayer of repentance for generational curses.
2. Command all affected valves to be healed.
3. Command all swollen veins to return to normal.

VENEREAL DISEASE (Also called VD or STDs.) (Also see AIDS.)

STDs are among the most common infectious diseases. Sexually Transmitted Diseases are infections that are passed from person to person through intimate sexual contact.

Some STD's are transmitted by kissing or by close body contact. The organisms responsible for other STD's (for example, HIV and hepatitis viruses) can be transmitted through non-sexual contact such as from mother to child at birth, through breastfeeding, and exposure to contaminated food, water, blood, medical instruments, or needles.

How to Minister: (All commands done in Jesus' name.)

1. Lead them in a prayer of repentance for ungodly covenants, if necessary.
2. Curse the root of the infection and/or virus and command it to go.
3. Command the immune system to function properly and be fully restored.
4. Command healing to any affected parts.
5. Lead them in a prayer of forgiveness, if necessary.
6. Lead them in a prayer to lay all cares, stress, and worries on the altar of God.
7. Lead them in a prayer of repentance for diet or lifestyle, if necessary.

VERTIGO (Also see Meniere's Disease.)

Dizziness is described as being unsteady, lightheaded, weakness, loss of balance, or Vertigo (a feeling that you or the room is spinning or moving).

Dizziness is usually not serious and either quickly resolves or is easily treated. However, dizziness can progress to Vertigo, which can be seriously disabling until symptoms disappear.

The most common causes of Vertigo are changing the position of the head too quickly, Labyrinthitis (inflammation of the inner ear), a viral infection of the inner ear, or Meniere's Disease. Vertigo can also bring on ringing in the ears and accompany or be exacerbated by nausea, vomiting, and/or migraine headaches.

How to Minister: (All commands done in Jesus' name.)
1. Lead in a prayer of repentance for generational curses.
2. Command the fluid in the ears to return to normal.
3. Command any infection to leave and the Vertigo to go and balance to return to normal.

WALLEYED (SEE CROSS-EYED.)

WARTS

Warts are small growths on the skin caused by a virus. They are generally harmless; however, they can be disfiguring or embarrassing. Common warts usually appear on the hands. Flat warts are usually found on the face and forehead. Genital warts are found in the pubic area, on or around the genitals, and in the area between the thighs. Plantar warts develop on the soles of the feet. Subungual and periungual warts appear under and around the fingernails or toenails

Most warts tend to cause no discomfort unless they are in areas of repeated friction or pressure. Plantar warts can become extremely painful and may cause problems with running and walking.

How to Minister: (All commands done in Jesus' name.)
1. Curse the seed of the root and command the wart to dry up and fall off.
2. Lead them in a prayer of repentance, if necessary.

WATER ON THE KNEE OR ELBOW (See Edema.)

WEBBING (See Floaters.)

WEST NILE VIRUS

Transmitted by mosquitoes, the West Nile Virus causes a mild to severe illness with mild flu-like symptoms. Severe forms of the disease can be life-threatening.

The West Nile Virus organism is similar to many other mosquito-borne viruses that are spread when a mosquito bites an infected bird and then bites a person.

Even though many people are bitten by mosquitoes that carry the West Nile Virus, only a few people develop or notice any symptoms.

How to Minister: (All commands done in Jesus' name.)

1. Curse the root of the disease and command it to go.
2. Command all prions to be discarded.
3. Command new blood and organs, if necessary.

WHIPLASH

Whiplash is an injury to the neck caused by a sudden jerking or "whipping" of the head. When a vehicle stops suddenly or is struck from behind, the seat belt keeps a person's body from being thrown forward. However, the head may snap forward, then backward, causing a Whiplash injury. In addition to car accidents, Whiplash can be caused by amusement park rides, sports injuries, or by being punched or shaken vigorously. Abuse is the suspected cause when this injury is found in young children.

How to Minister: (All commands done in Jesus' name.)

1. Curse the pain and command it to go.

2. Command the neck to come into alignment.
3. Command any damaged disc, vertebrae, nerve, ligament, tendon, or muscle to be healed.
4. Command the spirit of trauma to leave, if necessary.

YEAST INFECTIONS (See Candida.)

Index

Please Note: This Index is to assist you in finding specific conditions mentioned in Chapter 13. Items in all capital letters are major headings in Chapter 13 Prayers for Various Conditions. Items in upper and/or lower case are mentioned within other major headings.

A

B

F

G

H

M

n

O

P

Q

R

S

Other Prayers

About the Author

$\mathcal{J}$oan Hunter is a compassionate minister, dynamic teacher, accomplished author, and anointed healing evangelist who has devoted her life to carry a message of hope, deliverance, and healing to the nations. As founder and president of Joan Hunter Ministries, Hearts 4 Him, 4 Corners Foundation, and 4 Corners World Outreach Center, Joan's vision is to equip believers to take the healing power of God beyond the four walls of the church to the four corners of the earth.

Joan ministers the gospel with manifestations of supernatural signs and wonders in healing schools, miracle services, conferences, local churches, and revival centers around the world. She is sensitive to the move of the Spirit and speaks prophetically into services and individual lives of those in attendance. Joan's genuine approach and candid delivery enable her to connect intimately with people from all educational, social, and cultural backgrounds.

Joan Hunter brings a powerful ministry to a world characterized by brokenness and pain. Having emerged victorious through tragic circumstances, impossible obstacles, and immeasurable devastation, Joan is able to share a message of hope and restoration to the brokenhearted, deliverance and freedom to the bound, and healing and wholeness to the diseased. Joan's life is one of uncompromising dedication to the gospel of Jesus Christ, as she exhibits a sincere desire to see the body of Christ live free, happy, and whole.

At the tender age of twelve, Joan committed her life to Christ and began faithfully serving in ministry alongside her parents, Charles and Frances Hunter, as they traveled around the globe conducting Healing Explosions and Healing Schools. Prior to branching out into her own international healing ministry, Joan co-pastored a church for eighteen years.

Joan is the author of three books: *Healing the Whole Man Handbook* is an exhaustive guide for physical healing, providing key insights into the root causes of hundreds of diseases with step-by-step instructions on how to pray specifically for each; *Healing the Heart* is Joan's personal testimony from brokenness to wholeness, providing timeless insight for overcoming impossible situations; and her most recent book, *Power to Heal,* describes the path to complete health and teaches how God can use anyone to be the conduit of His supernatural healing to others.

Joan has ministered in miracle services and conducted healing schools in numerous countries around the world. She has also been the featured guest on many television and radio shows, including Sid Roth's *It's Supernatural!, It's a New Day, The Miracle Channel,* Steve Shultz's *Prophetic TV,* and many others. Joan's television appearances have been broadcast around the world on World Harvest Network, Inspiration Network, Daystar, Faith TV, Cornerstone TV, The Church Channel, and Total Christian Television, Christian Television Network, Watchmen Broadcasting, and God TV.

Joan and her husband, Kelley Murrell, live in Pinehurst, Texas. She has four grown daughters, her husband has four sons, and she is a blessed grandmother.